AF351045

All Things Work Together for Good

Register This New Book

Benefits of Registering*

- ✓ FREE **replacements** of lost or damaged books
- ✓ FREE **audiobook** – *Pilgrim's Progress,* audiobook edition
- ✓ FREE information about new titles and other **freebies**

www.anekopress.com/new-book-registration

*See our website for requirements and limitations.

All Things
Work Together
for Good

(Or, A Divine Cordial)

The Spiritual Privilege of Those Who
Love God and Are Savingly Called

Thomas Watson

Contents

A Divine Tonic

We know that all things work together for good to them that love God, to them who are the called according to his purpose.
—Romans 8:28

Christian Reader,
There are two things that I have always looked upon as difficult. The one is to make the wicked sad, and the other is to make the godly joyful. Dejection in the godly arises from a double spring: It is either because their inward comforts are darkened, or their outward comforts are disturbed.

To cure both of these troubles, I have written this book, hoping, by the blessing of God, that it will lift up their desponding hearts and make them look up with a more cheerful outlook. I would prescribe them to take, now and then, a little of this cordial, or healthful tonic: *All things work together for good to them that love God* (Romans 8:28).

To know that nothing hurts the godly is a matter of comfort, but to be assured that all things that happen will work together for their good, that their crosses will be turned into blessings, and that showers of affliction water the withering root of their grace and make it flourish more may fill their hearts with joy until they run over.

– Thomas Watson

Introduction

If the whole Scripture is the feast of the soul, as Ambrose said, then Romans 8 may be a dish at that feast, and with its sweet variety may very much refresh and animate the hearts of God's people. In the preceding verses, the apostle Paul had been wading through the great doctrines of justification and adoption – mysteries so difficult and profound that without the help and conduct of the Spirit, he might quickly have waded beyond his depth. In this verse the apostle touches upon that pleasant string of consolation: *We know that all things work together for good to them that love God* (Romans 8:28). Every word there is weighty; therefore, I will gather up every filing of this gold so that nothing will be lost.

In the text there are three general branches:

First, there is a glorious privilege. All things work for good.

Second, there are the people interested in this privilege. They are doubly specified. They are those who love God, and they are called.

Third, there is the origin and spring of this effectual calling, set down in these words: *according to his purpose* (Romans 8:28).

Regarding the glorious privilege, there are two things to be considered:

1. The certainty of the privilege: *We know.*

2. The excellence of the privilege: *All things work together for good.*

1. The certainty of the privilege: *We know.* It is not a matter that is uncertain or doubtful. The apostle does not say, "We hope" or "We suppose," but it is like an article in our creed: *We know that all things work together for good.* Therefore observe that the truths of the gospel are certain and infallible.

A Christian may reach not merely a vague opinion, but a certainty of what he believes. As sayings and proverbs are evident to reason, so the truths of Christianity are evident to faith. *We know,* says the apostle. Although a Christian does not have a perfect knowledge of the mysteries of the gospel, yet he has a certain knowledge. *We see through a glass, darkly* (1 Corinthians 13:12); therefore, we do not have perfection of knowledge, but we behold *with open face* (2 Corinthians 3:18). Therefore, we have certainty. The Spirit of God imprints heavenly truths upon the heart, as with the point of a diamond. A Christian may know infallibly that there is an evil in sin and a beauty in holiness. He may know that he is in the state of grace. *We know that we have passed from death unto life* (1 John 3:14).

He may know that he will go to heaven. *We know that if our earthly house of this tabernacle were dissolved, we have a building of God, an house not made with hands, eternal in the heavens* (2 Corinthians 5:1). The Lord does not leave His people at uncertainties in matters of salvation. The apostle says, *We know.* We have arrived at a holy assurance. We have both the Spirit of God, and our own experience, setting seal to it.

Let us then not rest in skepticism or doubts, but let us labor to come to a certainty in the things of Christianity. As that martyr woman said, "I cannot dispute for Christ, but I can burn for Christ."[1] God knows whether we may be called forth to be witnesses to His truth; therefore, it is important for us to be well grounded and confirmed in it. If we are doubting Christians, we will be wavering Christians. From where does apostasy come but from doubt? People first question the truth, and then fall from the truth. Oh, beg the Spirit of God not only to anoint you, but also to seal you (2 Corinthians 1:22).

2. The excellence of the privilege: *All things work together for good.* This is as Jacob's staff in the hand of faith, with which we may walk cheerfully to the mount of God.

What will satisfy or make us content if this will not? *All things work together for good.* This expression *work together* refers to medicine. Several poisonous ingredients put together, being diluted and adjusted by the skill of the apothecary, *God's providences being divinely tempered and sanctified work together for the best to the saints.* make a separate medicine and work together for the good of the patient. So all God's providences being divinely tempered and sanctified work together for the best to the saints. He who loves God and is called according to His purpose may rest assured that everything in the world will be for his good.

This is a Christian's gentle, healing tonic that may warm him and make him like Jonathan who, when he had tasted the honey at the end of the rod, *his eyes were enlightened* (1 Samuel 14:27).

---

1   This quote seems to be from the short book *An Account of the Last Words of Christian Ker Who Died at Edinburgh, on the 4th of February 1702, in the 11th Year of Her Age* by Archibald Dean (although not said by her, but listed by the author among some quotes by others who died a martyr's death.

Why should a Christian destroy himself? Why should he kill himself with concern and anxiety when all things will harmonize and sweetly work together for his good? The result of the text is this: All the various dealings of God with His children do, by a special providence, turn to their good. *All the paths of the LORD are mercy and truth unto such as keep his covenant and his testimonies* (Psalm 25:10). If every path has mercy in it, then it works for good.

Chapter 1

The Best Things Work for Good to the Godly

We will first consider what things work for good to the godly, and we will show here that both the best things and the worst things work for their good. We begin with the best things.

1. God's attributes work for good to the godly.

(1). God's power works for good. It is a *glorious power* (Colossians 1:11), and it is engaged for the good of the elect.

God's power works for good in supporting us in trouble. *Underneath are the everlasting arms* (Deuteronomy 33:27). What upheld Daniel in the lion's den? Jonah in the fish's belly? The three Hebrews in the furnace? Only the power of God. Is it not strange to see a bruised reed grow and flourish? How is a weak Christian able not only to endure affliction, but to rejoice in it? He is upheld by the arms of the Almighty. *My strength is made perfect in weakness* (2 Corinthians 12:9).

The power of God works for us by supplying our needs. God creates comforts when means fail. He who brought food to the prophet Elijah by ravens will bring sustenance to His people. God can preserve the oil in the jar (1 Kings 17:14). The Lord made the sun on Ahaz's dial go backward ten degrees (Isaiah 38:8); and when our outward comforts are declining, and the sun is almost setting, God often causes a revival and brings the sun many degrees backward.

The power of God subdues our corruptions. *He will subdue our iniquities* (Micah 7:19). Is your sin strong? God is powerful. He will break the head of this leviathan (Psalm 74:14). Is your heart hard? God will dissolve that stone in Christ's blood. *God maketh my heart soft* (Job 23:16). When we say as Jehoshaphat, *We have no might against this great company that cometh against us* (2 Chronicles 20:12), the Lord goes up with us and helps us to fight our battles. He strikes off the heads of those Goliath lusts that are too strong for us.

The power of God conquers our enemies. He spoils the pride and breaks the confidence of adversaries. *Thou shalt break them with a rod of iron* (Psalm 2:9). There is rage in the enemy and malice in the devil, but there is power in God. How easily He can defeat all the forces of the wicked! *Lord, it is nothing with thee to help* (2 Chronicles 14:11). God's power is on the side of His church. *Happy art thou, O Israel . . . , O people saved by the Lord, the shield of thy help, and who is the sword of thy excellency!* (Deuteronomy 33:29).

(2). The wisdom of God works for good. God's wisdom is our teacher to instruct us. As He is the mighty God, so He is also the *Counsellor* (Isaiah 9:6). We are oftentimes in the dark, and in matters that are complicated and unclear, we do not know which way to take. Then God comes in with light. *I will guide thee with mine eye* (Psalm 32:8). "Eye" there stands for God's wisdom. Why is it that the saints can see farther than the most sharp-sighted politicians? They foresee the evil, and they hide themselves; they see Satan's deceptions. God's wisdom is the pillar of fire to go before them and guide them.

(3). The goodness of God works for good to the godly. God's goodness is a means to make us good. *The goodness of God leadeth thee to repentance* (Romans 2:4). The goodness of God is a spiritual sunbeam to melt the heart into tears. "Oh," says the soul, "has God been so good to me? Has He spared me so long from hell, and will I grieve His Spirit anymore? Will I sin against goodness?"

The goodness of God works for good, as it ushers in all blessings.

The goodness of God works for good, as it ushers in all blessings. The favors we receive are the silver streams that flow from the fountain of God's goodness. This divine attribute of goodness brings in two types of blessings. (1) Common blessings: everyone shares in these, the bad as well as the good. This sweet dew falls upon the thistle as well as the rose. (2) Crowning blessings: Only the godly partake of these. *Who crowneth thee with lovingkindness and tender mercies* (Psalm 103:4). Thus, the blessed attributes of God work for good to the saints.

2. The promises of God work for good to the godly.

The promises are notes of God's hand. Is it not good to have security? The promises are the milk of the gospel. Is not the milk for the good of the infant? They are called *precious promises* (2 Peter 1:4). They are as refreshing liquids to a soul that is ready to faint. The promises are full of virtue.

Are we under the guilt of sin? There is a promise: *The LORD, the LORD God, merciful and gracious* (Exodus 34:6), where God as it were puts on His glorious embroidery and holds out the golden scepter to encourage poor trembling sinners to come to

Him. *The Lord God, merciful.* God is more willing to pardon than to punish. Mercy multiplies more in Him than sin does in us. Mercy is His nature. The bee naturally gives honey; it stings only when it is provoked.

"But," says the guilty sinner, "I cannot deserve mercy." Yet He is gracious. He shows mercy, not because we deserve mercy, but because He delights in mercy. But what is that to me? Perhaps my name is not in the pardon. He keeps *mercy for thousands* (Exodus 34:7). The treasury of mercy is not exhausted. God has treasures lying by, and why should you not come in for a child's portion?

Are we under the defilement of sin? There is a promise working for good: *I will heal their backsliding* (Hosea 14:4). God will not only bestow mercy, but He will also bestow grace. He has made a promise of sending His Spirit (Isaiah 44:3), which, for its sanctifying nature, is in Scripture compared sometimes to water, which cleanses the vessel; sometimes to the fan, which winnows corn and purifies the air; and sometimes to fire, which refines metals. Thus the Spirit of God will cleanse and consecrate the soul, making it partake of the divine nature.

Are we in great trouble? There is a promise that works for our good: *I will be with him in trouble* (Psalm 91:15). God does not bring His people into trouble and leave them there. He will stand by them. He will hold their heads and hearts when they are fainting. And there is another promise: *He is their strength in the time of trouble* (Psalm 37:39). "Oh," says the soul, "I will faint in the day of trial." But God will be the strength of our hearts. He will join His forces with us. Either He will make His hand lighter or our faith stronger.

Do we fear outward needs? There is a promise: *They that seek the Lord shall not want any good thing* (Psalm 34:10). If it is good for us, we will have it; if it is not good for us, then the withholding of it is good. *He shall bless thy bread, and thy water* (Exodus 23:25). This blessing falls as the honey dew upon the leaf; it sweetens that little we possess. Let me lack the venison so that I may have the blessing. But I fear I will not get a livelihood? Examine that verse: *I have been young, and now am old; yet have I not seen the righteous forsaken, nor his seed begging bread* (Psalm 37:25). How must we understand this? David speaks it as his own observation. He never beheld such a decline. He never saw a godly man brought so low that he did not have a bit of bread to put in his mouth. David never saw the righteous and their seed lacking. Though the Lord might test godly parents a while by lack, yet not their seed too; the seed of the godly will be provided for. David never saw the righteous begging bread and forsaken. Though he might be reduced to great difficulties, yet he is not forsaken. He is still an heir of heaven, and God loves him.

Question: How do the promises work for good?

Answer: They are food for faith – and that which strengthens faith works for good. The promises are the milk of faith; faith sips nourishment from them, as the child from the breast. *Jacob was greatly afraid and distressed* (Genesis 32:7). His spirit was ready to faint, but then he went to the promise: *Thou saidst, I will surely do thee good* (Genesis 32:12). This promise was his food. He got so much strength from this promise that he was able to wrestle with the Lord all night in prayer, and would not let Him go until He had blessed him.

The promises are also springs of joy. There is more in the promises to comfort than in the world to perplex. The reformer Caspar Ursinus was comforted by the promise: *No man is able to pluck them out of my Father's hand* (John 10:29). The promises are refreshing tonics in a fainting fit. *Unless thy law had been my delights, I should then have perished in my affliction*

(Psalm 119:92). The promises are as cork to the net, to lift up the heart from sinking in the deep waters of distress.

3. The mercies of God work for good to the godly.

The mercies of God humble. *Then went king David in, and sat before the* LORD, *and he said, Who am I, O Lord* GOD? *And what is my house, that thou hast brought me hitherto?* (2 Samuel 7:18). Lord, why is such honor bestowed upon me, that I should be king – that I who followed the sheep should go in and out before Your people? A gracious heart says, "Lord, what am I that it should be better with me than with others – that I should drink of the fruit of the vine when others drink not only a cup of wormwood, but a cup of blood [or suffering to death]? What am I that I should have those mercies that others want, who are better than I? Lord, why is it, that notwithstanding all my unworthiness, a fresh tide of mercy comes in every day?" The mercies of God make a sinner proud, but a saint humble.

The mercies of God have a melting influence upon the soul. They dissolve it in love for God. God's judgments make us fear Him, but His mercies make us love Him. How Saul was worked upon by kindness! David had him at the advantage, and could have cut off not only the hem of his robe, but his head; yet he spared his life. This kindness melted Saul's heart: *Is this thy voice, my son David? And Saul lifted up his voice, and wept* (1 Samuel 24:16). God's mercy has such a melting influence; it makes the eyes drop with tears of love.

The mercies of God make the heart fruitful. When you lay out more cost upon a field, it bears a better crop. A gracious soul honors the Lord with his substance. He does not do with his mercies, as Israel, with their jewels and earrings, make a golden calf; but, as Solomon did with the money thrown into the treasury, build a temple for the Lord. The golden showers of mercy cause fruitfulness.

The mercies of God make the heart thankful. *What shall I render unto the LORD for all his benefits toward me? I will take the cup of salvation, and call upon the name of the LORD* (Psalm 116:12–13). David alludes to the people of Israel, who at their peace offerings used to take a cup in their hands and give thanks to God for deliverances. Every mercy is a gift of free grace, and this enlarges the soul in gratitude. A good Christian is not a grave to bury God's mercies, but a temple to sing His praises. As Ambrose said, if every bird in its kind chirps forth thankfulness to its Maker, much more will a genuine Christian, whose life is enriched and fragranced with mercy.

Every mercy is a gift of free grace, and this enlarges the soul in gratitude.

The mercies of God invigorate. As they draw us to His love, so they sharpen our obedience. *I will walk before the LORD in the land of the living* (Psalm 116:9). He who reviews his blessings looks upon himself as a person active for God. He argues from the sweetness of mercy to the swiftness of duty. He spends and is spent for Christ. He dedicates himself to God. Among the Romans, when one had redeemed another, he was afterward to serve him. A soul encompassed with mercy is zealously active in God's service.

The mercies of God work compassion to others. A Christian is an earthly savior. He feeds the hungry, clothes the naked, and visits the widows and orphans in their distress. He sows among them the golden seeds of his charity. *A good man showeth favour, and lendeth* (Psalm 112:5). Charity drops from him freely, as myrrh from the tree. Thus to the godly, the mercies of God work for good. They are wings to lift them up to heaven.

Spiritual mercies also work for good.
The Word preached works for good. It is a savor of life. It is a soul-transforming Word. It assimilates the heart into Christ's

likeness. It produces assurance. *Our gospel came not unto you in word only, but also in power, and in the Holy Ghost, and in much assurance* (1 Thessalonians 1:5). It is the chariot of salvation.

Prayer works for good. Prayer is the bellows of the affection. It enlarges holy desires and passions of soul. Prayer has power with God. *Command ye me* (Isaiah 45:11). It is a key that unlocks the treasury of God's mercy. Prayer keeps the heart open to God, and closed to sin. It calms the unbridled hearts and increases of lust. It was Martin Luther's counsel to a friend, when he perceived a temptation begin to arise, to go pray. Prayer is the Christian's gun that he discharges against his enemies. Prayer is the sovereign medicine of the soul. Prayer sanctifies every mercy (1 Timothy 4:5). It dispels sorrow; by venting the grief, it eases the heart. When Hannah had prayed, she went away, *and her countenance was no more sad* (1 Samuel 1:18). And if it has these rare effects, then it works for good.

The Lord's Supper works for good. It is an emblem of the marriage supper of the Lamb (Revelation 19:9), and an assurance of that communion we will have with Christ in glory. It is a feast of good things. It gives us bread from heaven, that which preserves life and prevents death. It has glorious effects in the hearts of the godly. It stirs up their affections, strengthens their graces, crushes their corruptions, revives their hopes, and increases their joy. Martin Luther said, "It is as great a work to comfort a dejected soul as to raise the dead to life"; yet this may be done and sometimes is done to the souls of the godly in the blessed Supper.

4. The graces of the Spirit work for good.

Grace is to the soul as light is to the eye and as health is to the body. Grace does to the soul as a virtuous wife does to her husband: *She will do him good and not evil all the days of her life*

(Proverbs 31:12). How incomparably useful are the graces! Faith and fear go hand in hand. Faith keeps the heart cheerful, and fear keeps the heart serious. Faith keeps the heart from sinking in despair, and fear keeps it from floating in presumption. All the graces display themselves in their beauty: hope is *the helmet* (1 Thessalonians 5:8), meekness is *the ornament* (1 Peter 3:4), and love is *the bond of perfectness* (Colossians 3:14). The saints' graces are weapons to defend them, wings to elevate them, jewels to enrich them, spices to perfume them, stars to adorn them, and tonics to refresh them. Does not all this work for good? The graces are our evidences for heaven. Is it not good to have our evidences at the hour of death?

5. The angels work for the good of the saints.

The good angels are ready to help in all ministrations of love to the people of God. *Are they not all ministering spirits, sent forth to minister for them who shall be heirs of salvation?* (Hebrews 1:14). Some of the church fathers were of the opinion that every believer has his own guardian angel. This subject does not need any fierce debate. It is enough for us to know that the whole hierarchy of angels is employed for the good of the saints.

The good angels do service to the saints in life. The angel comforted the virgin Mary (Luke 1:28). The angel stopped the mouths of the lions so that they could not hurt Daniel (Daniel 6:22). A Christian has an invisible guard of angels around him: *He shall give his angels charge over thee, to keep thee in all thy ways* (Psalm 91:11). The angels help care for the saints in this life: *Are they not all ministering spirits?* (Hebrews 1:14). Even the highest angels take care of the lowest saints.

The good angels do service at death. The angels are around the saints' sickbeds to comfort them. As God comforts by His Spirit, so He also comforts by His angels. Christ in His agony was refreshed by an angel (Luke 22:43), and so are believers in the agony of death; and when the saints' breath expires, their souls are carried up to heaven by a convoy of angels (Luke 16:22).

The good angels also do service at the day of judgment. The angels will open the saints' graves and will conduct them into the presence of Christ, when they will be made like His glorious body. *He shall send his angels with a great sound of a trumpet, and they shall gather together his elect from the four winds, from the one end of heaven to the other* (Matthew 24:31). The angels at the day of judgment will rid the godly of all their enemies. Here in this world, the saints are plagued with enemies. *They . . . are mine adversaries; because I follow the thing that good is* (Psalm 38:20). Soon the angels will help to free God's people from all their enemies: *The tares are the children of the wicked one; the enemy that sowed them is the devil; the harvest is the end of the world; and the reapers are the angels. As therefore the tares are gathered and burned in the fire, so shall it be in the end of this world. The Son of man shall send forth his angels, and they shall gather out of his kingdom all things that offend, and them which do iniquity; and shall cast them into a furnace of fire* (Matthew 13:38-42). At the day of judgment, the angels of God will take the wicked, which are the tares, and will bundle them up and throw them into the furnace of hell, and then the godly will not be troubled with enemies anymore. Thus, the good angels work for good. See here the honor and dignity of a believer. He has God's name written upon him (Revelation 3:12), the Holy Spirit dwelling in him (2 Timothy 1:14), and a guard of angels attending him.

6. The communion of saints works for good.

We . . . are helpers of your joy (2 Corinthians 1:24). One Christian conversing with another is a means to strengthen him. As the stones in an arch help to strengthen one another, one Christian, by sharing his experience, warms and inspires another. *Let us . . . provoke one another unto love and to good works* (Hebrews 10:24). Grace flourishes much by holy discussion! A Christian by good discourse drops that oil upon another that makes the lamp of his faith burn brighter.

7. Christ's intercession works for good.

Christ is in heaven as Aaron was with his golden plate upon his forehead and his precious incense; and He prays for all believers as well as He did for the apostles. *Neither pray I for these alone, but for them also that shall believe on me through their word* (John 17:20). When a Christian is weak and can hardly pray for himself, Jesus Christ is praying for him; and He prays for three things. First, He prays that the saints may be kept from sin: *I pray . . . that thou shouldest keep them from the evil* (John 17:15). We live in the world

When Satan is tempting, Christ is praying!

as in a house of plague; Christ prays that His saints may not be infected with the contagious evil of the times. Second, He prays for His people's progress in holiness: *Sanctify them* (John 17:17). Let them have constant supplies of the Spirit and be anointed with fresh oil. Third, He prays for their glorification: *Father, I will that they also, whom thou hast given me, be with me where I am* (John 17:24). Christ is not content until the saints are in His arms. This prayer, which He made on earth, is the copy and pattern of His prayer in heaven. What a comfort this is! When Satan is tempting, Christ is praying! This works for good.

Christ's prayer takes away the sins of our prayers. Ambrose

compared this to a child who, wanting to present his father with a flower, goes into the garden, and there gathers some flowers and some weeds together; but coming to his mother, she picks out the weeds and puts the flowers together, and so it is presented to the father. And so when we have put up our prayers, Christ comes and picks away the weeds, the sin of our prayer, and presents nothing but flowers to His Father, which are a sweet-smelling savor.

8. The prayers of saints work for good to the godly.

The saints pray for all the members of the spiritual body. Their prayers prevail much. They prevail for recovery from sickness: *The prayer of faith shall save the sick, and the Lord shall raise him up* (James 5:15). The prayers of saints prevail for victory over enemies: *Lift up thy prayer for the remnant that is left* (Isaiah 37:4). *Then the angel of the Lord went forth, and smote in the camp of the Assyrians a hundred and fourscore and five thousand* (Isaiah 37:36). The prayers of saints prevail for deliverance out of prison: *Prayer was made without ceasing of the church unto God for him. . . . And, behold, the angel of the Lord came upon him, and a light shined in the prison: and he smote Peter on the side, and raised him up, . . . and his chains fell off* (Acts 12:5, 7). The angel brought Peter out of prison, but it was prayer that brought the angel. The prayers of saints prevail for forgiveness of sin: *My servant Job shall pray for you: for him will I accept* (Job 42:8).

Thus, the prayers of the saints work for good to the spiritual body of Christ. And this is no small privilege to a child of God, that he has a constant exchange of prayer exerted for him. When he comes into any place, he may say, "I have some prayer here; all over the world, I have a supply of prayer going for me. When I am unwell and am having difficulties, others are praying for me who are alert and strong." Thus, the best things work for good to the people of God.

The Worst Things Work for Good to the Godly

Do not mistake me. I am not saying that of their own nature the worst things are good, for they are a fruit of the curse; but although they are naturally evil, they are morally good due to the wise overruling hand of God disposing and sanctifying them. Although the elements are of contrary qualities, yet God has so molded them that they all work in a harmonious manner for the good of the universe. Or as with a watch: The wheels seem to move contrary to one another, but they all carry on the motions of the watch. So things that seem to move in opposition to the godly end up working for their good due to the wonderful providence of God. Among these worst things, there are four sad evils that work for good to those who love God.

1. The evil of affliction works for good to the godly.

It is a heart-calming consideration to know that in all the afflictions that visit us, God has a special hand in them: *The Almighty hath afflicted me* (Ruth 1:21). Instruments cannot act until God gives them an assignment any more than an axe can chop by itself without a hand. Job looked to God in his affliction. Therefore, as Augustine observed, he did not say, "The Lord gave, and the devil took away," but, *The Lord hath taken away* (Job 1:21). No matter who brings an affliction to us, it is God who sends it.

Another heart-calming consideration is that afflictions work for good. *Like these good figs, so will I acknowledge them that are carried away captive of Judah, whom I have sent out of this place into the land of the Chaldeans for their good* (Jeremiah 24:5). Judah's captivity in Babylon was for their good. *It is good for me that I have been afflicted* (Psalm 119:71). This text, like Moses' tree cast into the bitter waters of affliction, may make them sweet and wholesome to drink. Afflictions are restorative to the godly. God extracts our salvation out of the most poisonous drugs. Afflictions are as necessary as ordinances (1 Peter 1:6). No vessel can be made of gold without fire; so it is impossible for us to be made vessels of honor unless we are melted and refined in the furnace of affliction. *All the paths of the Lord are mercy and truth* (Psalm 25:10).

As the artist merges bright colors with dark shadows, so the wise God mixes mercy with judgment. Those troubling occurrences that seem to be detrimental are beneficial. Let us take some examples from Scripture. Joseph's brothers threw him into a pit. Afterward, they sold him. Then he was cast into prison; yet all this worked for his good. His difficulties made way for his advancement. He was made the second-highest man in the kingdom. *Ye thought evil against me; but God meant it unto good* (Genesis 50:20). Jacob wrestled with the angel, and the hollow of Jacob's thigh was put out of joint. This was sad, but God turned it to good, for there he saw God's face, and there the Lord blessed him. *Jacob called the name of the place Peniel: for I have seen God face to face* (Genesis 32:30). Who would not be willing to have a bone out of joint if he could then have a sight of God?

King Manasseh was bound in chains. This was sad to see – a crown of gold changed into chains of iron; but it worked for his good, for *when he was in affliction, he besought the* Lord *his God, and humbled himself greatly before the God of his fathers, and prayed unto him: and he was intreated of him, and heard his supplication* (2 Chronicles 33:12-13). He was more indebted to his iron chain than to his golden crown; the one made him proud, and the other made him humble.

Job was a spectacle of misery. He lost all that he ever had. He abounded only in boils and ulcers. This was sad, but it worked for his good. His grace was proved and improved. God gave a testimony from heaven of his integrity, and compensated his loss by giving him *twice as much as he had before* (Job 42:10).

The pains of affliction produce much good to those who love God.

Paul was struck with blindness. This was uncomfortable, but it turned to his good. By that blindness, God made a way for the light of grace to shine into his soul. It was the beginning of a happy conversion (Acts 9).

As the hard frosts in winter bring on the flowers in the spring, and as the night ushers in the morning star, so the pains of affliction produce much good to those who love God. However, we are ready to question the truth of this and to ask, as Mary asked the angel, "How can this be?" (Luke 1:34). Therefore, I will show you several ways how affliction works for good.

1. Afflictions act as our preacher and tutor: *Hear ye the rod* (Micah 6:9). Martin Luther said that he could never rightly understand some of the psalms until he was in affliction. Affliction teaches us what sin is. In the Word preached, we hear what a dreadful thing sin is – that it is both defiling and damning

– but we do not fear it any more than we fear a painted lion; therefore God lets loose affliction, and then we feel sin bitter in the fruit of it. A sickbed often teaches more than a sermon. We can best see the ugly countenance of sin in the mirror of affliction. Affliction teaches us to know ourselves. In prosperity, we are for the most part strangers to ourselves. God makes us know affliction so that we may better know ourselves. We see the corruption in our hearts in the time of affliction, which we otherwise would not believe was there. Water in the glass looks clear, but if you set it on the fire, the scum boils up. In prosperity, a man seems to be humble and thankful – the water looks clear; but set this man a little on the fire of affliction, and the scum boils up – much impatience and unbelief appear. "Oh," says a Christian, "I never thought I had as bad of a heart as I now see I have. I never thought my corruptions were so strong and my graces so weak."

2. Afflictions work for good, as they are the means of making the heart more upright. In prosperity, the heart is apt to be divided (Hosea 10:2). The heart clings partly to God and partly to the world. It is like a needle between two magnets: God draws, and the world draws. God then takes away the world so that the heart may cling more to Him in sincerity. Correction is setting the heart right and straight. As we sometimes hold a crooked rod over the fire to straighten it, so God holds us over the fire of affliction to make us straighter and more upright. Oh, how good it is, when sin has bent the soul away from God, that affliction would straighten it again!

3. Afflictions work for good, as they conform us to Christ. God's rod is a pencil to draw Christ's image more vividly upon us. It is good that there would be symmetry and proportion between the Head and the members. Would we be parts of

Christ's spiritual body, and not be like Him? His life, as John Calvin said, was a series of sufferings. He was *a man of sorrows, and acquainted with grief* (Isaiah 53:3). He wept and bled. Was His head crowned with thorns, and do we think we will be crowned with roses? It is good to be like Christ, even if it is by sufferings. Jesus Christ drank a bitter cup. It made Him sweat drops of blood to think of it; and, although it is true that He drank the poison in the cup (the wrath of God), yet there is some wormwood left in the cup, which the saints must drink. Here is the difference between Christ's sufferings and ours: His sufferings satisfied justice, while ours are only corrective.

4. Afflictions work for good to the godly, as they are destructive to sin. Sin is the mother, and affliction is the daughter; the daughter helps to destroy the mother. Sin is like the tree that breeds the worm, and affliction is like the worm that eats the tree. There is much corruption in the best heart. Affliction works it out by degrees, as the fire works out the dross from the gold. *This is all the fruit to take away his sin* (Isaiah 27:9). What does it matter if we have more of the rough file if it results in less rust? Afflictions carry away nothing but the dross of sin. If a physician would say to a patient, "Your body is unhealthy and is full of bad fluids that must be cleared out, or you will die; but I will prescribe medicine that, though it may make you sick, yet it will carry away the remnants of your disease and will save your life" – would not this be for the good of the patient? Afflictions are the medicine that God uses to carry away our spiritual diseases. They cure the swelling of pride, the fever of lust, and the excess of covetousness. Do they not then work for good?

5. Afflictions work for good, as they are the means of loosening our hearts from the world. When you dig away the dirt from

the root of a tree, it is to loosen the tree from the earth; and so God digs away our earthly comforts to loosen our hearts from the earth. A thorn grows up with every flower. God would have the world hang as a loose tooth which, being wiggled away, does not much trouble us. Is it not good to be weaned? The oldest saints need it. Why does the Lord break the conduit pipe except that we may go to Him, in whom are all our fresh springs (Psalm 87:7).

6. Afflictions work for good, as they make way for comfort. In the valley of Achor is a *door of hope* (Hosea 2:15). Achor signifies trouble. God sweetens outward pain with inward peace. *Your sorrow shall be turned into joy* (John 16:20). Here is the water turned into wine. After a bitter pill, God gives sugar. Paul had his prison songs. God's rod has honey at the end of it. The saints in weakness have had such sweet raptures of joy that they thought themselves in the borders of the heavenly Canaan.

7. Afflictions work for good, as they are a magnifying of us. *What is man, that thou shouldest magnify him? And that thou shouldest set thine heart upon him?* (Job 7:17). God, by affliction, magnifies us in three ways. (1) In that He will condescend so low as to take notice of us. It is an honor that God will notice dust and ashes. It is a magnifying of us that God thinks us worthy to be smitten. God not striking us is a slighting: *Why should ye be stricken any more?* (Isaiah 1:5). If you will continue in sin, take your course and sin yourselves into hell. (2) Afflictions also magnify us, as they are emblems of glory and signs of sonship. *If you endure chastening, God dealeth with you as with sons* (Hebrews 12:7). Every mark of the rod is a badge of honor. (3) Afflictions tend to the magnifying of the saints, as they make them distinguished in the world. Soldiers have never been so admired for their victories as the saints have been for

their sufferings. The zeal and constancy of the martyrs in their trials have rendered them famous to posterity. How eminent was Job for his patience! God leaves his name upon record: *Ye have heard of the patience of Job* (James 5:11). Job the sufferer was more renowned than Alexander the conqueror.

8. Afflictions work for good, as they are the means of making us happy. *Happy is the man whom God correcteth* (Job 5:17). What politician or moralist ever placed happiness in the cross? Job does: *Happy is the man whom God correcteth.*

It may be asked, "How do afflictions make us happy?" We reply that, being sanctified, they bring us nearer to God. The moon when full is farthest from the sun; so are many people farther away from God in the full moon of prosperity; afflictions bring them nearer to God. The magnet of mercy does not draw us as near to God as the cords of affliction. When Absalom set Joab's corn on fire, then he came running to Absalom (2 Samuel 15:30). When God sets our worldly comforts on fire, then we run to Him and make our peace with Him. When the prodigal was faced with need, then he returned home to his father (Luke 15). When the dove could not find any rest for the sole of her foot, then she flew to the ark (Genesis 8:9). When God brings a flood of affliction upon us, then we run to the ark of Christ. Thus affliction makes us happy in that it brings us nearer to God. Faith can make use of the waters of affliction to swim faster to Christ.

9. Afflictions work for good, as they put the wicked to silence. How ready they are to discredit and disparage the godly, saying that they serve God only for self-interest. Therefore, God will have His people endure sufferings for His religion so that He

may put a padlock on the lying lips of wicked people. When the atheists of the world see that God has a people who serve Him not for pay, but for love, this stops their mouths. The devil accused Job of hypocrisy, saying that he was a mercenary man and all his religion was made up of ends of gold and silver. *Doth Job fear God for naught? Hast not thou made an hedge about him?* (Job 1:9-10). "Well," said God, "put forth your hand and touch his belongings." As soon as the devil received permission, he began breaking down Job's hedge; but still Job worshipped God and professed his faith in Him (Job 1:20-21). *Though he slay me, yet will I trust in him* (Job 13:15). This silenced the devil himself. It strikes an obstacle into wicked men when they see that the godly will keep close to God in a suffering condition, and that, when they lose everything, they will still hold fast their integrity.

10. Afflictions work for good, as they make way for glory (2 Corinthians 4:17). It is not that they merit glory, but they prepare for it. As plowing prepares the earth for a crop, so afflictions prepare and make us ready for glory. The artist lays his gold upon dark colors, and so God first lays the dark colors of affliction, and then He lays the golden color of glory. The vessel is first seasoned before wine is poured into it, and the vessels of mercy are first seasoned with affliction before the wine of glory is poured in. Thus we see that afflictions are not detrimental to the saints, but beneficial. We should not so much look at the evil of affliction as the good, not so much at the dark side of the cloud as the light. The worst that God does to His children is to spur them on to heaven.

2. The evil of temptation is overruled
for good to the godly.

The evil of temptation works for good. Satan is called the tempter (Matthew 4:3). He is always lying in ambush, continually at work with one saint or another. The devil has his circuit that he walks every day. He is not yet fully cast into prison, but, like a prisoner who is out on bail, he walks around to tempt the saints. This is a great disturbance to a child of God. Concerning Satan's temptations, there are three things to be considered: (1) his method in tempting, (2) the extent of his power, and (3) that these temptations are overruled for good.

1. Satan's method in tempting. Take notice here of two things. His violence in tempting, and so he is the red dragon. He labors to storm the castle of the heart, he throws in thoughts of blasphemy, and he tempts people to deny God. These are the fiery darts he shoots, by which he tries to stir up the passions. Also notice his subtlety in tempting, and so he is the old serpent. There are five main subtleties that the devil uses:

1. He observes the temperament and character. He lays suitable baits of temptation. Like the farmer, he knows what grain is best for the soil. Satan will not tempt contrary to the natural disposition and temperament. This is his policy. He makes the wind and tide go together. The way the natural tide of the heart runs is the same way that the wind of temptation blows. Though the devil cannot know people's thoughts, yet he knows their temperament, and accordingly he lays his baits. He tempts the person eager for fame and power with a crown. He tempts others with beauty.

2. Satan observes the best time to tempt, just as a wise angler casts his hook when the fish will bite best. Satan's time of

tempting is usually after a Christian ordinance or when we feel near to God, and the reason is that he thinks he will find us most secure. When we have been at solemn duties, we are inclined to think that all is done, and we grow careless and are not as strict and determined as before – just as a soldier takes off his armor after a battle, not once dreaming of an enemy. Satan watches his time, and, when we least suspect, then he throws in a temptation.

3. He makes use of close relationships. The devil tempts by others. Thus he handed over a temptation to Job by his wife, who asked Job, *Dost thou still retain thine integrity?* (Job 2:9). A wife in the heart may be the devil's instrument to tempt to sin.

4. Satan tempts to evil by those who are good. He sometimes gives poison in a golden cup. He tempted Christ by Peter. Peter tried to prevent Him from suffering: *Be it far from thee, Lord: this shall not be unto thee* (Matthew 16:22). Who would have thought that the tempter would be found in the mouth of an apostle?

5. Satan tempts to sin under a pretense of religion. He is most to be feared when he transforms himself into an angel of light (2 Corinthians 11:14). He came to Christ with Scripture in his mouth: *It is written* (Matthew 4). The devil baits his hook with religion. He tempts many men to covetousness and extortion under a pretense of providing for their families. He tempts some people to do away with themselves so that they may live no longer to sin against God; so he draws them into sin under a pretense of avoiding sin. These are his subtle schemes in tempting.

2. The extent of his power; how far Satan's power in tempting reaches.

1. He can propose the object, as he set a wedge of gold before Achan (Joshua 7).

2. He can poison the imagination and instill evil thoughts into the mind. As the Holy Spirit casts in good suggestions, so the devil casts in bad ones. He put it into Judas' heart to betray Christ (John 13:2).

3. Satan can excite and provoke the corruption within, and work some kind of inclination in the heart to embrace a temptation. Though it is true that Satan cannot force the will to yield consent, yet he, being a resolute suitor, may provoke to evil by his continual pleadings. Thus he provoked David to number the people (1 Chronicles 21:1). The devil may, by his subtle arguments, argue us into sin.

3. These temptations are overruled for good to the children of God. A tree that is shaken by the wind is more settled and rooted, and the blowing of a temptation settles a Christian even more in grace. Temptations are overruled for good in eight ways:

1. Temptation sends the soul to prayer. The more furiously Satan tempts, the more fervently the saint prays. The deer that has been shot with an arrow runs faster to the water. When Satan shoots his fiery darts at the soul, it then runs faster to the throne of grace. When the messenger of Satan afflicted Paul, he said, *For this thing I besought the Lord thrice, that it might depart from me* (2 Corinthians 12:8). Temptation is a medicine for security. That which makes us pray more works for good.

2. Temptation to sin is a means to keep us from the commission of sin. The more a child of God is tempted, the more

he fights against the temptation. The more Satan tempts to blasphemy, the more a saint trembles at such thoughts and says, "Get away from me, Satan." When Joseph's master's wife tempted him to sin, the stronger her temptation was, the stronger his opposition was (Genesis 39). That temptation that the devil uses as a spur to sin, God makes as a bridle to keep back a Christian from it.

3. Temptation works for good, as it lessens the swelling of pride. *Lest I should be exalted above measure . . . , there was given me a thorn in the flesh, the messenger of Satan to buffet me* (2 Corinthians 12:7). The thorn in the flesh was to puncture the puffing up of pride. Better is that temptation that humbles me than that duty that makes me proud. Rather than allow a Christian to be proud-minded, God will let him fall into the devil's hands awhile to be cured of his corruption.

4. Temptation works for good, as it is a test to try what is in the heart. The devil tempts so that he may deceive, but God allows us to be tempted so He may try us. Temptation is a trial of our sincerity. When we can look a temptation in the face and turn our back upon it, it argues that our heart is pure and loyal to Christ. Also, it is a trial of our courage. *Ephraim also is like a silly dove without heart* (Hosea 7:11). It may be said of many people that they are without a heart; they have no heart to resist temptation. No sooner does Satan come, but they yield – like a coward who, as soon as the thief approaches, gives him his wallet. But he who brandishes the sword of the Spirit against Satan, and will rather die than yield, he is the courageous Christian. The courage of the Romans was never seen more than when they were attacked by the Carthaginians. The valor and strength of a saint is

never seen more than on a battlefield when he is fighting the red dragon, and by the power of faith puts the devil to flight. That grace is tried as gold that can stand in the fiery trial and withstand fiery darts.

5. Temptations work for good, as God makes those who are tempted able to comfort others in the same distress. A Christian must himself be under the assaults of Satan before he can speak a word in due season to those who are weary. Paul was familiar with temptations. *We are not ignorant of his devices* (2 Corinthians 2:11). Therefore, he was able to acquaint others with Satan's cursed schemes (1 Corinthians 10:13).

The child who is sick and bruised is most looked after.

A man who has ridden over a place where there are bogs and quicksands is best able to guide others through that dangerous way. He who has felt the claws of the roaring lion and has lain bleeding under those wounds is the right man to deal with one who is tempted. None can better reveal Satan's schemes and policies than those who have been long in the school of temptation.

6. Temptations work for good, as they stir up fatherly compassion in God to those who are tempted. The child who is sick and bruised is most looked after. When a saint lies under the bruising of temptations, Christ prays and God the Father shows compassion. When Satan puts the soul into a fever, God comes with a tonic. This made Martin Luther say that temptations are Christ's embraces because He then most sweetly reveals Himself to the soul.

7. Temptations work for good, as they make the saints long more for heaven. There they will be out of gunshot. Heaven is a place of rest. No bullets of temptation fly there. The eagle that soars aloft in the air and sits upon high trees

is not troubled with the sting of the serpent. In the same way, when believers are ascended to heaven, they will not be molested by the old serpent. In this life, when one temptation is over, another comes. This is to make God's people wish for death – to sound a retreat and call them off the field where the bullets fly so quick, to receive a victorious crown where not the drum and cannon, but the harp and viol will be always heard.

8. Temptations work for good, as they engage the strength of Christ. Christ is our friend, and when we are tempted, He sets all His power working for us. *For in that he himself hath suffered being tempted, he is able to succour them that are tempted* (Hebrews 2:18). If a poor soul was to fight alone with the Goliath of hell, he would be sure to be defeated, but Jesus Christ brings in His auxiliary forces and gives fresh supplies of grace. *We are more than conquerors through him that loved us* (Romans 8:37). Thus the evil of temptation is overruled for good.

Question: But sometimes Satan overthrows a child of God. How does this work for good?

Answer: I agree that a saint may be overcome through the suspension of divine grace and the fury of a temptation, yet this defeat by a temptation will be overruled for good. By this defeat, God makes way for the increase of grace. Peter was tempted to self-confidence. He stood upon his own strength, and when he needed to stand alone, Christ let him fall. But this worked for his good. It cost him many tears. *He went out, and wept bitterly* (Matthew 26:75). Then he grew more modest. He dared not say that he loved Christ more than the other apostles did. *Lovest thou me more than these?* (John 21:15). He dared not say so, for his fall had broken the neck of his pride.

The defeat by a temptation causes more circumspection and watchfulness in a child of God. Though Satan did lure him into sin before, yet for the future he will be more cautious. He will take care not to come within the lion's chain anymore. He is more shy and fearful of the occasions of sin. He never goes out without his spiritual armor, and he puts on his armor with prayer. He knows he walks on slippery ground, and therefore he looks wisely to his steps. He keeps close watch in his soul, and when he sees the devil coming, he stands to his arms and displays the shield of faith (Ephesians 6:16).

This is all the harm the devil does. When he defeats a saint by temptation, he cures him of his careless neglect. He makes him watch and pray more. When wild beasts get over the hedge and hurt the corn, a man will make his fence even stronger; and when the devil gets over the hedge by a temptation, a Christian will be sure to mend his fence. He will become more fearful of sin and more careful of duty. Thus, being beaten by temptation works for good.

Objection: But if being defeated works for good, this may make Christians careless whether they are overcome by temptations or not.

Answer: There is a great deal of difference between falling into a temptation and running into a temptation. Falling into a temptation will work for good, not running into it. He who falls into a river is capable of help and compassion, but he who purposefully turns into it is guilty of his own death. It is madness to run into a lion's den. He who runs himself into a temptation is like Saul, who fell upon his own sword (1 Samuel 31:4).

From all that has been said, see how God disappoints the old serpent, making his temptations turn to the good of His people. Surely if the devil knew how much benefit results to the saints by temptation, he would refrain from tempting. Martin Luther once said, "There are three things that make a Christian: prayer, meditation, and temptation." Paul, in his voyage to Rome, met with a contrary wind (Acts 27:4). The wind of temptation is a contrary wind to that of the Spirit, but God makes use of this crosswind to blow the saints to heaven.

3. The evil of desertion works for good to the godly.

The evil of desertion works for good. The spouse complains of desertion. *My beloved had withdrawn himself, and was gone* (Song of Solomon 5:6). There is a twofold withdrawing. There is a withdrawing in regard to grace, when God suspends the influence of His Spirit and withholds the living workings of grace. If the Spirit is gone, grace freezes into coldness and inactivity. There is also a withdrawing in regard to comfort. When God withholds the sweet manifestations of His favor, He does not look with such a pleasant aspect, but veils His face, and seems to be quite gone from the soul.

God is just in all His withdrawings. We desert Him before He deserts us. We desert God when we discontinue close communion with Him, when we desert His truths and dare not appear for Him, when we leave the guidance and conduct of His Word and follow the deceitful light of our own corrupt affections and passions. We usually desert God first; therefore, we have no one to blame but ourselves.

Desertion is very sad, for just as darkness follows when the light is withdrawn, so there is darkness and sorrow in the soul when God withdraws. Desertion is an agony of conscience. God holds the soul over hell. *The arrows of the Almighty are within me, the poison whereof drinketh up my spirit* (Job 6:4). It was a custom among the Persians in their wars to dip their arrows in the poison of serpents to make them more deadly.

Thus did God shoot the poisoned arrow of desertion into Job, under the wounds of which his spirit lay bleeding. In times of desertion, the people of God tend to be downcast. They argue against themselves and think that God has entirely cast them aside. Therefore, I will suggest some comfort to the deserted soul. The sailor, when he has no star to guide him, still has light in his lantern, which is some help to him to see his compass. I, then, will lay down four comforts, which are as the sailor's lantern, to give some light when the poor soul is sailing in the dark of desertion and wants the bright morning star.

1. None but the godly are capable of desertion. Wicked people do not know what God's love means, nor what it is to lack it. They know what it is to lack health, friends, and business, but they do not know what it is to lack God's favor. You fear you are not God's child because you are deserted. The Lord cannot be said to withdraw His love from the wicked, because they never had it. Being deserted is evidence that you are a child of God. How could you complain that God has alienated Himself if you had not sometimes received smiles and signs of love from Him?

   Wicked people do not know what God's love means, nor what it is to lack it.

2. There may be the seed of grace where there is not the flower of joy. The earth may want a crop of corn, yet may have a mine of gold within. A Christian may have grace within although the sweet fruit of joy does not grow. Vessels at sea that are richly full of jewels and spices may be in the dark and tossed in the storm. A soul enriched with the treasures of grace may still be in the dark of desertion, and so tossed as to think it will be cast away in the storm. David, in a state of dejection, prayed, *Take not thy Holy*

Spirit from me (Psalm 51:11). Augustine said that he did not pray, "Lord, give me Your Spirit," but "Do not take away Your Spirit," showing that the Spirit of God still remained in him.

3. These desertions are only for a time. Christ may withdraw and leave the soul awhile, but He will come again. *In a little wrath I hid my face from thee for a moment; but with everlasting kindness will I have mercy on thee* (Isaiah 54:8). When the tide is at its lowest, it will come in again. *I will not contend for ever, neither will I be always wroth: for the spirit should fail before me, and the souls which I have made* (Isaiah 57:16). The tender mother sets down her child in anger, but she will take him up again into her arms and kiss him. God may put away the soul in anger, but He will take it up again into His dear embraces, and display the banner of love over it.

4. These desertions work for good to the godly. Desertion cures the soul of sloth. We find the spouse fallen upon the bed of sloth: *I sleep* (Song of Solomon 5:2), and Christ was quickly gone: *My beloved had withdrawn himself* (Song of Solomon 5:6). Who will speak to one who is drowsy?

Desertion cures excessive affection for the world. *Love not the world* (1 John 2:15). We may hold the world as a flower in our hand, but it must not lie too near our heart. We may use it as an inn where we eat a meal, but it must not be our home. Perhaps these secular things steal away the heart too much. Good people are sometimes sick with excess, and drunk with the delicious delights of prosperity; and having spotted their silver wings of grace, and much defaced God's image by rubbing it against the earth, the Lord, to recover them of this, hides His face in a cloud. This eclipse has good effects. It darkens all the glory of the world and causes it to disappear.

Desertion works for good, as it makes the saints treasure God's countenance more than ever. *Thy lovingkindness is better than life* (Psalm 63:3). However, the commonness of this mercy lessens it in our esteem. When pearls became common at Rome, they began to be disregarded. God has no better way to make us value His love than by withdrawing it awhile. If the sun shone only once a year, how would it be treasured! When the soul has been long darkened with desertion, how welcome is the return of *the Sun of righteousness* (Malachi 4:2)!

Desertion works for good, as it is the means of making sin bitter to us. Can there be a greater misery than to have God's displeasure? What makes hell, but the hiding of God's face? And what makes God hide His face, but sin? *They have taken away my Lord, and I know not where they have laid him* (John 20:13). So our sins have taken away the Lord, and we do not know where He is laid. The favor of God is the best jewel. It can sweeten a prison and take away the sting of death. Oh, how revolting, then, is sin, which robs us of our best jewel! Sin made God desert His temple (Ezekiel 8:6). Sin causes Him to appear as an enemy and clothe Himself in armor. This makes the soul pursue sin with a holy malice and seek to be avenged of it. The deserted soul gives sin gall and vinegar to drink, and, with the spear of mortification, lets out its heart-blood.

Desertion works for good, as it sets the soul to weeping for the loss of God. When the sun is gone, the dew falls; and when God is gone, tears drop from the eyes. How Micah was troubled when he had lost his gods! *Ye have taken away my gods . . . , and what have I more?* (Judges 18:24). So when God is gone, what else do we have? The harp and viol cannot comfort us when God is gone. Although it is sad to lack God's presence, yet it is good to lament His absence.

Desertion sets the soul to seeking after God. When Christ was departed, the spouse pursued after Him. She sought Him in the streets of the city (Song of Solomon 3:2), and not having found Him, she made a shout and cried after Him: *Saw ye him whom my soul loveth?* (Song of Solomon 3:3). The deserted soul sends up whole volleys of sighs and groans. It knocks at heaven's gate by prayer. It can have no rest until the golden beams of God's face shine.

Desertion puts the Christian upon inquiry. He inquires about the reason for God's departure. What is the accursed thing that has made God angry (Joshua 7:1)? It might be pride, opposition to the ordinances, or worldliness. *For the iniquity of his covetousness was I wroth, and smote him: I hid me* (Isaiah 57:17). Perhaps there is some secret sin allowed. A stone in the pipe hinders the flow of water, and sin lived in hinders the sweet flow of God's love. Thus conscience, as a bloodhound, having found out sin and overtaken it – this Achan is stoned to death (Joshua 7).

Desertion works for good, as it gives us a sight of what Jesus Christ suffered for us. If the sipping of the cup is so bitter, how bitter was that which Christ drank upon the cross? He drank a cup of deadly poison, which made Him cry out, *My God, my God, why hast thou forsaken me?* (Matthew 27:46). None can so appreciate Christ's sufferings and be so kindled with love for Christ as those who have been humbled by desertion and have been held over the flames of hell for a time.

Desertion works for good, as it prepares the saints for future comfort. The chilling frosts prepare for spring flowers. It is God's way to first cast down, and then to comfort (2 Corinthians 7:6). When our Savior had been fasting, then came the angels and ministered to Him. When the Lord has kept His people fasting for a while, then He sends the Comforter and feeds them with the hidden manna. *Light is sown for the righteous* (Psalm 97:11). The saints' comforts may be hidden like seed under the ground, but the seed is ripening and will increase and flourish into a crop.

These desertions work for good, as they will make heaven sweeter to us. Here our comforts are like the moon: sometimes they are in the full, sometimes in the wane. God shows Himself to us awhile, and then retires from us. This will set apart heaven even more, and make it more delightful and captivating, when we will have a constant expression of love from God (1 Thessalonians 4:17).

Thus we see that desertions work for good. The Lord brings us into the deep of desertion so that He may not bring us into the deep of damnation. He puts us into a seeming hell so that He may keep us from a real hell. God is making us ready for that time when we will enjoy His smiles forever, when there will be neither clouds in His face or setting sun, when Christ will come and stay with His spouse, and the spouse will never again say, *My beloved [has] withdrawn himself* (Song of Solomon 5:6).

4. The evil of sin works for good to the godly.

Sin in its own nature is damnable, but God, in His infinite wisdom, overrules it and causes good to arise from that which seems most to oppose it. Indeed, it is a matter of wonder that any honey should come out of this lion (Judges 14:9). We may understand it in a double sense.

1. The sins of others are overruled for good to the godly. It is difficult for a gracious heart to live among the wicked. *Woe is me, that I sojourn in Mesech* (Psalm 120:5). Yet even this the Lord turns to good.

    1. The sins of others work for good to the godly, as they produce holy sorrow. God's people weep for what they cannot reform. *Rivers of waters run down mine eyes, because they*

keep not thy law (Psalm 119:136). David mourned for the sins of the times; his heart was turned into a spring, and his eyes into rivers. Wicked people rejoice in sin. *When thou doest evil, then thou rejoicest* (Jeremiah 11:15). But the godly are weeping doves; they grieve for the sins and blasphemies of the age. The sins of others, like spears, pierce their souls. This grieving for the sins of others is good. It shows a childlike heart, resenting with sorrow the injustices done to our heavenly Father. It also shows a Christlike heart. Jesus was *grieved for the hardness of their hearts* (Mark 3:5). The Lord takes special notice of these tears. He is pleased that we would weep when His glory suffers. It indicates more grace to grieve for the sins of others than for our own. We may grieve for our own sins out of fear of hell, but to grieve for the sins of others is from a principle of love for God. These tears drop as water from the roses. They are sweet and fragrant, and God puts them in His bottle (Psalm 56:8).

2. The sins of others work for good to the godly, as they move them more to pray against sin. If there were not such a spirit of wickedness around, perhaps there would not be such a spirit of prayer. Crying sins cause crying prayers. The people of God pray against the iniquity of the times, that God will give a hindrance to sin, that those committing sin will be ashamed. If they cannot pray down sin, they pray against it; and God takes this kindly. These prayers will be both recorded and rewarded. Even if we do not prevail in prayer, we will not lose our prayers. *My prayer returned into mine own bosom* (Psalm 35:13).

3. The sins of others work for good, as they make us more in love with grace. The sins of others are a veneer to set off the luster of grace even more. One contrary thing

sets off another. Deformity sets off beauty. The sins of the wicked much disfigure them. Pride is a disfiguring sin, and beholding another's pride makes us more in love with humility! Malice is a disfiguring sin; it is the devil's picture. The more of this we see in others, the more we love meekness and charity. Drunkenness is a disfiguring sin; it turns people into beasts and deprives them of the use of reason. The more intemperate we see others, the more we must love sobriety. The dark face of sin sets off the beauty of holiness so much more.

4. The sins of others work for good, as they work in us stronger opposition against sin. *They have made void thy law. Therefore I love thy commandments* (Psalm 119:126-127). David would have never loved God's law so much if the wicked had not set themselves so much against it. The more violent others are against the truth, the more valiant the saints are for it. Vigorous fish swim against the stream. The more the tide of sin comes in, the more the godly swim against it. The impieties of the times provoke holy passions in the saints. That anger is without sin that is against sin. The sins of others are as a whetstone to set the sharper edge upon us; they sharpen our zeal and indignation against sin even more.

5. The sins of others work for good, as they make us more fervent in working out our salvation. When we see wicked people take such efforts for hell, this makes us more industrious for heaven. The wicked have nothing to encourage them, yet they sin. They risk shame and disgrace. They break through all opposition. Scripture is against them, and conscience is against them. There is a flaming sword in the way, yet they sin. Godly hearts, seeing the wicked thus obsessed for the forbidden fruit, and

wearing out themselves in the devil's service, are more determined and inspired in the ways of God. They will take heaven as if by storm (Matthew 11:12). The wicked are swift dromedaries in sin (Jeremiah 2:23). And do we crawl like snails in religion? Will impure sinners do the devil more service than we do for Christ? Will they rush bolder to a prison than we do to a kingdom? Are they never weary of sinning, and are we weary of praying? Do we not have a better Master than they? Are not the paths of virtue pleasant? Is there not joy in the way of duty, and heaven at the end? The activity of the sons of Belial in sin is motivation to the godly to make them quicken their pace and run faster to heaven.

6. The sins of others work for good, as they are mirrors in which we may see our own hearts. Do we see a wicked, impious sinner? Behold a picture of our hearts. Such would we be if God would leave us. What is in other people's practice is in our nature. Sin in the wicked is like fire on a beacon that flames and blazes forth; sin in the godly is like fire in the embers. Christian, although you do not break forth into a flame of scandal, yet you have no cause to boast, for there is much sin swept up in the embers of your nature. You have the root of bitterness in you, and would bear as much hellish fruit as anyone if God did not either restrain you by His power or change you by His grace.

7. The sins of others work for good, as they are the means of making the people of God more thankful. When you see another person infected with the plague, how thankful you are that God has preserved you from it! The sins of others may be made of good use to make us more thankful. Why might not God have left us to the same *excess of*

riot (1 Peter 4:4)? Consider, O Christian, why should God be more favorable to you than to another? Why should He take you out of the wild olive tree of nature, and not someone else? This should make you adore free grace. What the Pharisee said boastingly, we may say thankfully: *God, I thank thee, that I am not as other men are, extortioners, unjust, adulterers, or even as this publican* (Luke 18:11). So we should adore the riches of grace that we are not as others – as drunkards, swearers, sabbath-breakers, etc. Every time we see people rushing on in sin, we are to thank God that we are not such. If we see an insane person, we thank God that it is not so with us. Much more when we see others under the power of Satan, we should make our thankful acknowledgement that it is not our condition. Let us not think lightly of sin.

8. The sins of others work for good, as they are means of making God's people better. Christian, God can make you gain by another person's sin. The more unholy others are, the more holy you should be. The more a wicked person gives himself to sin, the more a godly person gives himself to prayer. *But I give myself unto prayer* (Psalm 109:4).

9. The sins of others work for good, as they give an occasion to us of doing good. If there were no sinners, we could not be in such a position for service. The godly are often the means of converting the wicked. Their wise advice and pious example is a lure and a bait to draw sinners to embrace the gospel. The disease of the patient works for the good of the physician; by emptying the patient of toxic fluids, the physician enriches himself. By converting sinners from the error of their way, our crown is enlarged. *They that be wise shall shine as the brightness of*

the firmament; and they that turn many to righteousness as the stars for ever and ever (Daniel 12:3). They are not merely as lamps or candles, but are as the stars forever. So we see that the sins of others are overruled for our good.

2. The sense of their own sinfulness will be overruled for the good of the godly. Thus, our own sins will work for good. It must be understood carefully when I say that the sins of the godly work for good, for there is not the least good in sin. Sin is like poison; it corrupts the blood, infects the heart, and, without a sovereign antidote, brings death. This is the venomous nature of sin. It is deadly and damning. Sin is worse than hell, yet God, by His mighty overruling power, makes sin in the end turn to the good of His people. Hence that golden saying of Augustine: "God would never permit evil if He could not bring good out of evil." The feeling of sinfulness in the saints works for good in several ways.

1. Sin makes them weary of this life. It is sad that sin is in the godly, but it is good that it is a burden to them. Paul's afflictions (pardon the expression) were but a trifle to him in comparison with his sin. He rejoiced in tribulation (2 Corinthians 7:4), but this bird of paradise wept and grieved himself under his sins! *Who shall deliver me from the body of this death?* (Romans 7:24). A believer carries his sins as a prisoner wears his shackles. Oh, how he longs for the day of release! This sense of sin is good.

2. This indwelling of corruption makes the saints treasure Christ more. He who feels his sin, as a sick man feels his sickness – how welcome is Christ the physician to him! He who feels himself stung with sin – how precious is the bronze serpent to him! When Paul had mourned his body of death, how thankful he was for Christ! *I thank*

God through Jesus Christ our Lord (Romans 7:25). Christ's blood saves from sin, and it is the sacred ointment that cleanses us.

3. This sense of sin works for good in that it is an occasion of prompting the soul to undertake six specific duties:

a. It puts the soul upon self-searching. A child of God, being conscious of sin, takes the candle and lantern of the Word, and searches into his heart. He desires to know the worst of himself, just as a person who is diseased in body desires to know the worst of his disease. Although our joy lies in the knowledge of our graces, yet there is some benefit in the knowledge of our corruptions. Therefore Job prayed, *Make me to know my transgression and my sin* (Job 13:23). It is good to know our sins so that we may not flatter ourselves or think that we are better than we are. It is good to find out our sins before they find us out.

It is good to find out our sins before they find us out.

b. The indwelling of sin puts a child of God upon self-abasing. Sin is left in a godly person, as a cancer in the breast or a hunch upon the back, to keep him from being proud. Gravel and dirt are good to ballast a ship and keep it from overturning. The sense of sin helps to ballast the soul so that it is not overturned with vainglory. We read of the *spots* of God's children (Deuteronomy 32:5). When a godly person beholds his face in the mirror of Scripture, and sees the spots of unfaithfulness and hypocrisy, this makes the plumes of pride fall. They are humbling spots. It is a good use that may be made even of our sins when they bring about low thoughts of ourselves. The sin that humbles me is better than the duty that makes me proud. Holy

John Bradford uttered these words of himself: "I am a painted hypocrite"; and John Hooper said, "Lord, I am hell, and You are heaven."

c. Sin puts a child of God on self-judging. He passes a sentence upon himself. *I am more brutish than any man* (Proverbs 30:2). It is dangerous to judge others, but it is good to judge ourselves. *If we would judge ourselves, we should not be judged* (1 Corinthians 11:31). When a man has judged himself, Satan is put out of office. When he lays anything to a saint's charge, he is able to respond and say, "It is true, Satan. I am guilty of these sins, but I have already judged myself for them; and having condemned myself in the lower court of conscience, God will acquit me in the upper court of heaven."

d. Sin puts a child of God upon self-conflicting. One's spiritual self conflicts with one's carnal self. The Spirit lusts against the flesh (Galatians 5:17). Our life is a wayfaring life, and a warfaring life. There is a duel fought every day between the two seeds. A believer will not let sin have peaceable possession. If he cannot keep sin out, he will keep sin under; though he cannot quite overcome, yet he is overcoming. *To him that overcometh* (Revelation 2:7).

e. Sin puts a child of God upon self-observing. He knows that sin is a constant traitor, and therefore he carefully observes himself. A subtle heart needs a watchful eye. The heart is like a castle that is in danger every hour of being assaulted. This makes a child of God to always be a sentinel and keep a guard about his heart. A believer has a strict eye over himself so that he does not fall into any disgraceful sin, and so open a floodgate to let all his comfort run out.

f. Sin puts the soul upon self-reforming. A child of God does not only find out sin, but he drives out sin. He sets one foot upon the neck of his sins, and the other foot he turns to God's testimonies (Psalm 119:59). Thus the sins of the godly work for good. God makes the saints' maladies their medicines.

But let no one abuse this doctrine. I do not say that sin works for good to an unrepentant person. No, it works for his damnation, but it works for good to those who love God; and for you who are godly, I know you will not draw a wrong conclusion from this, either to make light of sin or to be bold in sin. If you should do so, God will make it cost you dearly. Remember David. He dared to sin presumptuously, and what did he get? He lost his peace. He felt the terrors of the Almighty in his soul, even though he had all aids to cheerfulness. He was a king and he had skill in music, yet nothing could give comfort to him. He complained of his "broken bones" (Psalm 51:8). And although he did eventually come out of that dark cloud, yet some theologians and clergymen are of the opinion that he never recovered his full joy to his dying day. If any of God's people would be meddling with sin because God can turn it to good, although the Lord does not damn them, He may send them to hell in this life. He may put them into such bitter agonies and attacks of soul that may fill them full of horror and make them draw near to despair. Let this be a flaming sword to keep them from coming near the forbidden tree.

And thus have I shown that both the best things and the worst things, by the overruling hand of the great God, work together for the good of the saints.

Again, I say, do not think lightly of sin.

Chapter 3

Why All Things Work for Good

1. The primary reason why all things work for good is the near and dear interest that God has in His people.

The Lord has made a covenant with them. *They shall be my people, and I will be their God* (Jeremiah 32:38). By virtue of this compact, all things do, and must, work for good to them. *I am God, even thy God* (Psalm 50:7). This word, *thy God*, is the sweetest word in the Bible. It implies the best relationship, and it is impossible for there to be such a relationship between God and His people and not have everything work for their good. This expression, "I am thy God," implies the following:

1. The relationship of a physician: "I am your Physician." God is a skillful physician. He knows what is best. God observes the different temperaments of men, and He knows what will work most effectively. Some people are of a sweeter disposition and are drawn by mercy. Others are more rugged and rough, and God deals with these people in a more forceful way. Some things are kept in sugar, and some in brine. God does not deal in the same way with all people. He has trials for the strong and tonics for the weak. God is a faithful physician, and therefore will work all things out for the best. If God does not give you that which

you like, He will give you that which you need. A physician does not so much study to please the taste of the patient as to cure his disease. We complain that very bitter trials lie upon us. Let us remember that God is our physician, and therefore He labors to heal us rather than coddle us. God's dealings with His children, although they are sharp, yet they are safe and are intended to cure so that He might *do thee good at thy latter end* (Deuteronomy 8:16).

2. This word, *thy God*, implies the relationship of a Father. A father loves his child; therefore, whether it is a smile or discipline, it is for the good of the child. "I am your God, your Father; therefore, everything I do is for your good." *As a man chasteneth his son, so the LORD thy God chasteneth thee* (Deuteronomy 8:5). God's chastening is not to destroy, but to reform. God cannot hurt His children, for He is a tenderhearted Father. *Like as a father pitieth his children, so the LORD pitieth them that fear him* (Psalm 103:13). Will a father seek the ruin of his child, the child who came from himself, who bears his image? All his care and planning are for his child; whom does he settle the inheritance upon, but his child? God is the tenderhearted *Father of mercies* (2 Corinthians 1:3). He brings about all the mercies and kindness in the creatures.

God is an *everlasting Father* (Isaiah 9:6). He was our Father from eternity. Before we were children, God was our Father, and He will be our Father to eternity. A father provides for his child while he lives; but the father dies, and then the child may be exposed to suffering and distress. But God never ceases to be a Father. You who are a believer have a Father who never dies; and if God is your father, you can never be ruined. All things must necessarily work for your good.

3. This word, *thy God*, implies the relation of a husband. This is a close and sweet relationship. The husband seeks the good of his spouse. It would be unnatural for him to go about to destroy his wife. *No man ever yet hated his own flesh* (Ephesians 5:29). There is a marriage relationship between God and His people. *Thy Maker is thine husband* (Isaiah 54:5). God entirely loves His people. He engraves them upon the palms of His hands (Isaiah 49:16). He sets them as a seal upon His heart (Song of Solomon 8:6). He will give kingdoms for their ransom (Isaiah 43:3). This shows how near they lie to His heart. If He is a husband whose heart is full of love, then He will seek the good of His spouse. Either He will shield off a wrong, or will turn it to the best.

4. This word, *thy God*, implies the relation of a friend. *This is my friend* (Song of Solomon 5:16). As Augustine said, a friend is half of oneself. He is thoughtful and desirous how he may do his friend good; he promotes his welfare as his own. Jonathan risked the king's displeasure for his friend David (1 Samuel 19:4). God is our friend. Therefore, He will turn all things to our good. There are false friends. Christ was betrayed by a friend; but God is the best friend.

He is a faithful friend. *Know therefore that the Lord thy God, he is God, the faithful God* (Deuteronomy 7:9). He is faithful in His love. He gave His very heart to us when He gave the Son out of His heart. This was a pattern of love without a parallel. He is faithful in His promises. *God, that cannot lie, promised* (Titus 1:2). He may change His promise, but He cannot break it. He is faithful in His dealings. When He is afflicting, He is faithful. *Thou in faithfulness hast afflicted me* (Psalm 119:75). He is sifting and refining us as silver (Psalm 66:10).

God is an immutable friend. *I will never leave thee, nor*

forsake thee (Hebrews 13:5). Friends often fail in difficult times. Many people deal with their friends as women do with flowers: while they are fresh, they gladly display them; but when they begin to wither, they throw them away. Many people deal with friends as the traveler does with the sundial: if the sun shines upon the dial, the traveler will step out of the road and look at it; but if the sun does not shine upon it, he will ride by and never take any notice of it. In the same way, if prosperity shines on people, then friends will look upon them; but if there is a cloud of adversity on them, they will not come near them. However, God is a friend forever. He has said, *I will never leave thee.* Though David walked in the shadow of death, he knew he had a friend by him: *I will fear no evil: for thou art with me* (Psalm 23:4). God never takes His love entirely away from His people. *He loved them unto the end* (John 13:1). God being such a friend will make all things work for our good. There is no true friend who will not seek the good of his friend.

5. This word, *thy God*, implies yet a nearer relationship – the relationship between the Head and the members. There is a spiritual union between Christ and the saints. He is called *the head of the church* (Ephesians 5:23). Does not the head desire what is good for the body? The head guides the body, it sympathizes with it, it is the fountain of spirits, and it sends forth influence and comfort into the body. All the parts of the head are placed for the good of the body. The eye is set, as it were, in the watchtower; it stands guard to notice any danger that may come to the body, and prevent it. The tongue is both a taster and an orator. If the body is a microcosm, or little world, then the head is the sun in this world from which proceeds the light of reason. The head is placed for the good of the body. Christ and the saints make one spiritual body. Our Head is in heaven, and certainly He will not allow His body to be hurt, but will

have regard for its safety and will make all things work for the good of the spiritual body.

2. Inferences from the proposition that all things work for the good of the saints.

1. If all things work for good, then we learn that there is a providence. Things do not work of themselves, but God sets them working for good. God is the great disposer of all events and matters. He sets everything working. *His kingdom ruleth over all* (Psalm 103:19). This is referring to His providential kingdom. Things in the world are not governed by second causes, by the counsels of men, or by the stars and planets, but by divine providence. Providence is the queen and governess of the world. There are three things in providence: God's foreknowing, God's determining, and God's directing all things to their periods and events. Whatever things work in the world, God sets them working. We read in the first chapter of Ezekiel about wheels, eyes in the wheels, and the moving of the wheels. The wheels are the whole universe, the eyes in the wheels are God's providence, and the moving of the wheels is the hand of Providence turning all things here below. That which is called chance by some people is nothing else but the result of God's providence.

Learn to adore providence. Providence has an influence upon all things here below. It is this that mingles the ingredients and makes up the whole compound.

2. Observe the happy condition of every child of God. All things, the best and worst things, work for his good. *Unto the upright there ariseth light in the darkness* (Psalm 112:4). The most dark and cloudy providences of God have some sunshine in them. What a blessed condition a true believer is in! When

he dies, he goes to God; and while he lives, everything will do him good. Affliction is for his good. What harm does the fire do to the gold? It only purifies it. What harm does the winnowing fan do to the corn? It only separates the chaff from it. God never uses His staff except to beat out the dust. Affliction does that which the Word many times will not; it opens the ear to discipline (Job 36:10). When God lays people upon their backs, then they look up to heaven. God smiting His people is like the musician striking upon the violin, which makes it put forth a melodious sound.

How much good comes to the saints by affliction! When they are pounded and broken, they send forth their sweetest smell. Affliction is a bitter root, but it bears sweet fruit. *It yieldeth the peaceable fruits of righteousness* (Hebrews 12:11). Affliction is the highway to heaven; though it is rough and thorny, yet it is the best way. Poverty will starve our sins. Sickness will make grace more helpful (2 Corinthians 4:16). Reproach will cause *the Spirit of glory and of God* to rest upon us (1 Peter 4:14). Death will stop the bottle of tears and open the gate of Paradise. A believer's dying day is his ascension day to glory. Because of that, the saints have put their afflictions in the inventory of their riches (Hebrews 11:26). Themistocles was banished from his own country, but he afterward grew in favor with the king of Egypt, whereupon he said, "I had perished, if I had not perished." So may a child of God say, "If I had not been afflicted, I would have been destroyed. If my health and possessions had not been lost, my soul would have been lost."

3. See, then, what an encouragement it is to become godly. All things will work for good. Oh, that this may persuade the world to fall in love with true religion! Can there be a greater attraction to piety? Can anything more prevail with us to be

good than this – that all things will work for our good? The Christian religion is the true alchemist's stone that turns everything into gold. Take the sourest part of religion, the suffering part, and there is comfort in it. God sweetens suffering with joy. He sweetens our wormwood with sugar. Oh, how may this persuade us to godliness! *Acquaint now thyself with [God], and be at peace: thereby good shall come unto thee* (Job 22:21). No one ever lost by his acquaintance with God. By this, good will come unto you – abundance of good, the sweet distillations of grace, the hidden manna. Yes, everything will work for good. Oh, then get acquainted with God and promote His interest.

4. Notice the miserable condition of wicked people. To those who are godly, evil things work for good; to those who are evil, good things work for harm.

1. Earthly good things work for harm to the wicked. Riches and prosperity are not benefits, but snares, as Seneca says. Worldly things are given to the wicked, as Michal was given to David, for a snare (1 Samuel 18:21). The vulture is said to draw sickness from a perfume, and so do the wicked from the sweet perfume of prosperity. Their mercies are like poisoned bread given to dogs. Their tables are sumptuously spread, but there is a hook under the bait: *Let their table become a snare* (Psalm 69:22). All their enjoyments are like Israel's quails, which were seasoned with the wrath of God (Numbers 11:33). Pride and luxury are the twins of prosperity. *Thou art waxen fat.... Then he forsook God* (Deuteronomy 32:15). Riches are not only like the spider's web – unprofitable, but are like the cockatrice's egg – harmful. *Riches kept for the owners thereof to their hurt* (Ecclesiastes 5:13). The common mercies wicked people have are not magnets to draw them nearer to God, but are millstones to sink them

deeper in hell (1 Timothy 6:9). Their delicious delicacies are like Haman's banquet; after all their lordly feasting, death will bring in the bill, and they must pay it in hell.

2. Spiritual good things work for harm to the wicked. They suck poison from the flower of heavenly blessings.

The ministers of God work for their harm. The same wind that blows one ship to the haven blows another ship upon a rock. The same breath in the ministry that blows a godly man to heaven blows a profane sinner to hell. Those who come with the word of life in their mouths are yet a savor of death to many (2 Corinthians 2:16). *Make the heart of this people fat, and make their ears heavy* (Isaiah 6:10). The prophet was sent with a sad message, to preach their funeral sermon. Wicked people are worse for preaching. *They hate him that rebuketh in the gate* (Amos 5:10). Sinners grow more resolved in sin. Let God say what He will, they will do what they want. *As for the word that thou hast spoken unto us in the name of the LORD, we will not hearken unto thee* (Jeremiah 44:16). The word preached is not healing, but hardening. How dreadful it is for people to be doomed to hell with sermons!

Prayer works for their harm. *The sacrifice of the wicked is an abomination to the LORD* (Proverbs 15:8). A wicked person is in much difficulty: if he does not pray, he sins; if he does pray, he sins. *Let his prayer become sin* (Psalm 109:7). It would be a sad judgment if all the food a person ate would turn to nauseous fluid and breed diseases in the body, but that is how it is with a wicked person. The prayer that should do him good works for his harm. He prays against sin and sins against his prayer. His duties are tainted with atheism, impaired with hypocrisy. God abhors them.

The Lord's Supper works for their hurt. *Ye cannot drink the cup of the Lord, and the cup of devils: ye cannot be partakers of the Lord's table, and of the table of devils. Do we provoke the Lord to jealousy?* (1 Corinthians 10:21-22). Some professing Christians kept their idol feasts, yet would come to the Lord's table. The apostle says, "Do you provoke the Lord to wrath?" Profane people feast with their sins, yet will come to feast at the Lord's table. This is to provoke God. To a sinner there is death in the cup. He eats and drinks *damnation to himself* (1 Corinthians 11:29). Thus the Lord's Supper works for hurt to unrepentant sinners. After the sop, the devil entered (John 13:27).

Christ Himself works for harm to desperate sinners. He is *a stone of stumbling, and a rock of offence* (1 Peter 2:8). He is that because of the depravity of people's hearts; for instead of believing in Him, they are offended at Him. The sun, though in its own nature is pure and pleasant, yet it is hurtful to sore eyes. Jesus Christ is set for the fall and the rising of many (Luke 2:34). Sinners stumble at a Savior and pluck death from the tree of life. As strong medicine helps some patients but destroys others, so the blood of Christ is medicine to some people and is con-demnation to others. This is the unparalleled misery of those who live and die in sin. The best things work for their harm, and tonics themselves kill.

5. See here the wisdom of God, who can make the worst things imaginable turn to the good of the saints. He can, by divine chemistry, extract gold out of dross. *O the depth of the riches both of the wisdom and knowledge of God!* (Romans 11:33). It is God's great design to set forth the wonder of His wisdom. The Lord made Joseph's prison a step to promotion. There was no way for Jonah to be saved except by being swallowed up. God

allowed the Egyptians to hate Israel (Psalm 106:41), and this was the means of their deliverance. Paul was bound with a chain, and that chain that bound him was the means of furthering the gospel (Philippians 1:12). God enriches by impoverishing. He causes the increase of grace by the decrease of an estate. When the creature goes further from us, it is that Christ may come nearer to us.

God works uncommonly. He brings order out of confusion, and harmony out of discord. He frequently makes use of unjust people to do that which is just. *He is wise in heart* (Job 9:4). He can reap His glory out of men's fury (Psalm 76:10). Either the wicked will not do the harm that they intend, or they will do the good that they do not intend. God often helps when there is the least hope, and saves His people in a way that they think will destroy. He made use of the high priest's malice and Judas' treason to redeem the world. Through indiscreet emotion, we tend to find fault with things that happen. This is as if an illiterate person would censure philosophy, or a blind person would find fault with the work in a landscape. *Vain men would be wise* (Job 11:12). Foolish creatures will be accusing Providence, and calling the wisdom of God to the court of reason. God's ways are *past finding out* (Romans 11:33). They are rather to be admired than understood. There is never a providence of God that does not have either a mercy or a wonder in it. How amazing and infinite that wisdom is that makes the most adverse dispensations work for the good of His children!

6. Learn how little cause we have, then, to be discontented at outward trials and emergencies! What! Discontented at that which will do us good! All things will work for good. There are no sins that God's people are more subject to than unbelief

and impatience. They are ready either to faint through unbelief or to agonize through impatience. When people speak out against God because of discontentment and impatience, it is a sign that they do not believe this text. Discontentment is an ungrateful sin because we have more mercies than afflictions; and it is an irrational sin because afflictions work for good. Discontentment is a sin that puts us upon sin. *Fret not thyself . . . to do evil* (Psalm 37:8). He who frets will be ready to do evil. Fretting Jonah was sinning Jonah (Jonah 4:9). The devil blows the coals of passion and discontentment, and then warms himself at the fire. Oh, let us not nourish this angry viper in our hearts. Let this text produce patience: *All things work together for good to them that love God* (Romans 8:28). Will we be discontented at that which works for our good? If one friend would throw a bag of money at another, and in throwing it, would graze his head, he would not be troubled much since by this means he had received a bag of money. So the Lord may bruise us by afflictions, but it is to enrich us. These afflictions work for us a *weight of glory* (2 Corinthians 4:17), and will we be discontented?

7. See here that Scripture fulfilled: *God is good to Israel* (Psalm 73:1). When we look upon adverse providences, and see the Lord covering His people with ashes and making them *drunken with wormwood* (Lamentations 3:15), we may be ready to call in question the love of God and to say that He deals harshly with His people. But, oh no – God is still good to Israel, because He makes all things work for good. Is not He a good God who turns all to good? He works out sin, and works in grace; is not this good? *We are chastened of the Lord, that we should not be condemned with the world* (1 Corinthians 11:32). The depth of affliction is to save us from the depth of damnation. Let us

always side with God; when our outward condition is ever so bad, let us say, "Yet God is good."

8. See what cause the saints have to be constant in the work of thanksgiving. Christians are defective in this. Even though they may be much in supplication, yet they are often little in expressing thanks. The apostle Paul says, *In everything give thanks* (1 Thessalonians 5:18). Why? Because God makes everything work for our good. We thank the physician, even though he gives us a bitter medicine that makes us sick, because it is to make us well. We thank anyone who does something good for us, and will we not be thankful to God, who makes everything work for good to us?

God loves a thankful Christian. Job thanked God when He took everything away: *The Lord hath taken away; blessed be the name of the Lord* (Job 1:21). Many people will thank God when He gives, but Job thanked Him when He took away – because he knew that God would work good out of it. We read of saints with harps in their hands (Revelation 14:2), an emblem of praise. We meet many Christians who have tears in their eyes and complaints in their mouths, but there are few who have harps in their hands and who praise God in affliction. To be thankful in affliction is a work unique to a saint. Every bird can sing in spring, but some birds will sing in the dead of winter. Everyone, almost, can be thankful in prosperity, but a true saint can be thankful in adversity. A good Christian will bless God not only at sunrise, but also at sunset. Well may we, in the worst that happens to us, have a psalm of thankfulness – because all things work for good. Oh, be much in thanking God; we will thank Him who befriends us.

9. Consider that if the worst things work for good to a believer, what will the best things do – Christ and heaven! How much

more will these work for good! If the cross has so much good in it, what has the crown? If such precious clusters grow in Golgotha, how delicious is the fruit that grows in Canaan? If there is any sweetness in the waters of Marah, what is there in the wine of Paradise? If God's rod has honey at the end of it, what has His golden scepter? If the bread of affliction tastes so savory, what is manna? What is the heavenly nectar? If God's discipline and afflictions work for good, what will the smiles of His face do? If temptations and sufferings have matters of joy in them, what will glory have? If there is so much good out of evil, what then is that good where there will be no evil? If God's chastening mercies are so great, what will His crowning mercies be? Wherefore comfort one another with these words.

10. Consider that if God makes all things to turn to our good, how right it is that we should make all things turn to His glory! *Do all to the glory of God* (1 Corinthians 10:31). The angels glorify God; they sing divine anthems of praise. How then we should glorify Him, for whom God has done more than for angels! He has dignified us above them in uniting our nature with the Godhead. Christ has died for us, and not the angels. The Lord has given us not only out of the common provisions of His bounty, but He has enriched us with covenant blessings, and He has bestowed upon us His Spirit. He studies our wellbeing, and He makes everything work for our good. Free grace has laid a plan for our salvation. If God seeks our good, will we not seek His glory?

Question: How can we be said to properly glorify God? He is infinite in His perfections, and can receive no increase from us.

Answer: It is true that in a strict sense we cannot bring glory to God, but in an evangelical sense we may. When we do what lies in us to lift up God's name in the world, and to cause others to have high and reverential thoughts of God, the Lord interprets this as glorifying Him, just as a person is said to dishonor God when he causes the name of God to be evil spoken of.

We are said to advance God's glory in three ways: (1) When we work toward His glory. We advance God's glory when we make Him the first and the last in our thoughts and in our purpose. As all the rivers run into the sea, and all the lines meet in the center, so all our actions culminate and center in God. (2) We advance God's glory by being fruitful in grace. *Herein is my Father glorified, that ye bear much fruit* (John 15:8). Barrenness reflects dishonor upon God. We glorify God when we grow in fairness as the lily, in tallness as the cedar, and in fruitfulness as the vine. (3) We glorify God when we give the praise and glory of all we do unto God. There was a king of Sweden who gave an excellent and humble speech when he feared that the people would ascribe glory to him that was due to God, and would cause him to be removed before the work was done. When the silkworm weaves her curious work, she hides herself under the silk and is not seen. When we have done our best, we must vanish away in our own thoughts and transfer the glory of all to God. The apostle Paul said, *I laboured more abundantly than they all* (1 Corinthians 15:10). One would think that this speech savored of pride, but the apostle pulled off the crown from his own head and set it upon the head of free grace: *Yet not I, but the grace of God which was with me.* Constantine used to write the name of Christ over the door, and so should we over our duties.

Let us then endeavor to make the name of God glorious and renowned. If God seeks our good, let us seek His glory. If He makes all things tend to our edification, let us make all things tend to His exaltation.

Chapter 4

Of Love for God

I proceed to the second general branch of the text: the people interested in this privilege. They love God. *All things work together for good to them that love God* (Romans 8:28).

Despisers and haters of God have no lot or part in this privilege. It is children's bread. It belongs only to those who love God. Because love is the very heart and spirit of the Christian religion, I will more fully discuss this. For the further discussion of it, let us notice these five things concerning love for God:

1. The nature of love for God. Love is an expansion of soul, or the kindling of the affections, by which a Christian breathes after God as the supreme and sovereign good. Love is to the soul as the weights to the clock. It sets the soul in motion toward God, as the wings by which we fly to heaven. By love we cling to God, as the needle to the magnet.

2. The basis of love for God – knowledge. We cannot love that which we do not know. In order for our love to be drawn forth to God, we must know these three things in Him:

1. A fullness (Colossians 1:19). He has a fullness of grace

to cleanse us, and of glory to crown us. It is a fullness not only of sufficiency, but of abundance. He is a sea of goodness without bottom and banks.

2. A freeness. God has an innate propensity to dispense mercy and grace. He drips goodness as the honeycomb. *Whosoever will, let him take the water of life freely* (Revelation 22:17). God does not require us to bring money with us, only an appetite.

3. A propriety, or property. We must know that this fullness in God is ours. *This God is our God* (Psalm 48:14). The foundation of love is His deity and the interest we have in Him.

3. The kinds of love, which I will split into these three:

1. There is a love of appreciation. When we set a high value upon God as being the most sublime and infinite good, we so esteem God as that if we have Him, we are content even if we lack everything else. The stars vanish when the sun appears. All creatures vanish in our thoughts when the Sun of righteousness shines in His full splendor.

2. A love of contentment and delight – as a person takes delight in a friend whom he loves. The soul that loves God rejoices in Him as in his treasure, and rests in Him as in his center. The heart is so set upon God that it desires no more. *Show us the Father, and it sufficeth us* (John 14:8).

3. A love of benevolence – which is wishing well to the cause of God. He who is endeared in affection to his friend wishes all happiness to him. We love God when we are well-wishers. We desire that His interest may prevail. Our vote and prayer is that His name may be had in honor; that His gospel, which is the rod of His strength, may, like Aaron's rod, blossom and bring forth fruit.

4. The properties of love.

1. Our love for God must be entire and must be with the whole heart. *Thou shalt love the Lord thy God with all thy heart* (Mark 12:30). In the old law, a high priest was not to marry a widow or a harlot. He was not to marry a widow because he was not her first love. He was not to marry a harlot because he did not have all her love. God will have the whole heart. *Their heart is divided* (Hosea 10:2). The true mother would not have the child divided (1 Kings 3:26), and God will not have the heart divided. God will not be a mere occupant, to have only one room in the heart, with all the other rooms rented out to sin. It must be an entire love.

   Our love for God must be entire and must be with the whole heart.

2. It must be a sincere love. *Grace be with all them that love our Lord Jesus Christ in sincerity* (Ephesians 6:24). "Sincere" alludes to honey that is quite pure. Our love for God is sincere when it is pure and without self-interest. The scholars call this a love of friendship. We must love Christ, as Augustine says, for Himself, just as we love sweet wine for its taste. God's beauty and love must be the two magnets that draw our love to Him. Alexander had two friends – Hephestion and Craterus – of whom he said, "Hephestion loves me because I am Alexander; Craterus loves me because I am King Alexander." The one loved his person, and the other loved his gifts. Many people love God because He gives them corn and wine (Genesis 27:28; Joel 2:19), and not for His intrinsic excellencies. We must love God more for what He is than for what He gives. True love is not greedy. You do not need to pay a mother to love her child. A soul deeply in love

with God does not need to be hired with rewards. It cannot but love Him for that luster of beauty that sparkles forth in Him.

3. It must be a fervent love. The Hebrew word for love signifies intensity of affection. Saints must be seraphim, burning in holy love. To love someone coldly is the same as not to love him. The sun shines as hot as it can. Our love for God must be intense and fervent, like coals of juniper, which are most intense and strong (Psalm 120:4). Our love for temporary things must be indifferent; we must love as if we loved not (1 Corinthians 7:30). But our love for God must flame forth. The spouse was sick with love for Christ (Song of Solomon 2:5). We can never love God as He deserves. Just as God's punishing us is less than we deserve (Ezra 9:13), so our loving Him is less than He deserves.

4. Love for God must be active. It is like fire, which is the most active element. It is called the labor of love (1 Thessalonians 1:3). Love is no idle grace; it sets the head studying for God, and the feet running in the ways of His commandments. *The love of Christ constraineth us* (2 Corinthians 5:14). Pretenses of love are insufficient. True love is not only seen at the tongue's end, but at the finger's end; it is the labor of love. The living creatures mentioned in Ezekiel 1:8 had wings – an emblem of a good Christian. He not only has the wings of faith to fly, but he has hands under his wings. He works by love, and he spends and is spent for Christ.

5. Love is generous and unselfish. It has signs of love to bestow (1 Corinthians 13:4). Love is kind. Love has not only a smooth tongue, but it has a kind heart. David's heart was fired with love for God, and he would not offer

that to God which cost him nothing (2 Samuel 24:24). Love is not only full of benevolence, but also compassion. Love that enlarges the heart never limits the hand. He who loves Christ will be compassionate to His members. He will be eyes to the blind and feet to the lame. The backs and bellies of the poor will be the furrows in which he sows the golden seeds of compassion. Some people say that they love God, but their love is limited to one hand; they give nothing to good uses. Indeed, faith deals with invisibles, but God hates the love that is invisible. Love is like new wine, which will have vent; it emits itself in good works. The apostle Paul speaks in honor of the Macedonians, that they gave to the poor saints, not only up to, but *beyond their power* (2 Corinthians 8:3). Love is cultivated at court; it is a noble, compassionate grace.

6. Love for God is distinct. He who loves God gives Him a kind of love that he gives to no one else. Just as God gives His children a kind of love that He does not bestow upon the wicked (electing, adopting love), so a gracious heart gives to God a special, distinguishing love that no one else can share in. *I have espoused you to one husband, that I may present you as a chaste virgin to Christ* (2 Corinthians 11:2). A wife married to one husband gives him a kind of love that she has for no one else. She does not part with her wedded love to anyone but her husband. In the same way, a saint pledged to Christ gives Him a distinct kind of love, a love inexpressible to anyone else. It is a love joined with adoration. Not only is love given to God, but the soul is given to Him as well. *A garden enclosed is my sister, my spouse* (Song of Solomon 4:12). The heart of a believer is Christ's garden. The flower growing in it is love mixed with divine worship, and this flower

is for the use of Christ alone. The spouse keeps the key of the garden so that none may go there except Christ.

7. Love for God is permanent. It is like the fire that the vestal virgins kept at Rome; it does not go out. True love boils over, but does not stop. Love for God, as it is sincere and without hypocrisy, is also constant without apostasy. Love is like the pulse of the body; it is always beating. It is not a land, but a spring flood. Wicked people are constant in love to their sins. Neither shame, nor sickness, nor fear of hell will make them stop their sins. In the same way, nothing can hinder a Christian's love for God. Nothing can conquer love – not any difficulties or opposition. *Love is strong as death* (Song of Solomon 8:6). The grave swallows up the strongest bodies, and love swallows up the strongest difficulties. *Many waters cannot quench love* (Song of Solomon 8:7) – not the sweet waters of pleasure or the bitter waters of persecution. Love for God abides firm until death. *Being rooted and grounded in love* (Ephesians 3:17). Light things, such as chaff and feathers, are quickly blown away; but a tree that is rooted abides the storm. He who is rooted in love endures. True love never ends, except with the life.

5. The degree of love. We must love God above all other objects. *There is none upon earth that I desire beside thee* (Psalm 73:25). God is the essence of all good things. He is superlatively good. The soul sees a special greatness in God, and admires in Him that constellation of all excellencies, and so is carried out in love to Him in the highest degree. Bernard said that the measure of our love for God must be to love Him without measure. God, who is the best of our happiness, must have the best of our affections. The creature may have the milk of our love, but

God must have the cream. Love for God must be above all other things, as the oil swims above the water.

We must love God more than we love our family members. We see an example of this in the case of Abraham offering up Isaac. Isaac was the son of his old age. There is no question that he loved him entirely and cherished him, but when God told Abraham to offer up his son (Genesis 22:2), he obeyed – even though it was something that might seem to oppose not only his reason, but also his faith, for the Messiah was to come from Isaac; and if he were cut off, from where would the world have a Mediator? Yet such was the strength of Abraham's faith and fervency of his *We must love God more than our possessions.* love for God that he was willing to take the sacrificing knife and let out Isaac's blood. Our blessed Savior speaks of hating father and mother (Luke 14:26). Christ would not want us to be unnatural, but if our dearest relations stand in our way and would keep us from Christ, either we must step over them or know them not (Deuteronomy 33:9). Although some drops of love may run beside us to our family and friends, yet the full torrent must run out after Christ. Relatives may lie *on* the heart, but Christ must lie *in* the heart.

We must love God more than our possessions. You *took joyfully the spoiling of your goods* (Hebrews 10:34). They were glad that they had anything to lose for Christ. If the world would be placed on one scale, and Christ on the other, He must weigh heaviest. And is it so? Does God have the highest place in our affections? Plutarch said, "When a dictator was created in Rome, all other authority was for the time suspended." So when the love of God bears sway in the heart, all other love is suspended, and is as nothing in comparison of this love.

Application: This is a sharp reproof to those who do not love God. This may serve as a sharp reproof to those who do not have a drop of love for God in their hearts – and are there such wretches alive? He who does not love God is a beast with a human head. Oh, wretch! Do you live upon God every day, yet not love Him? If someone had a friend who supplied him continually with money, and gave him all that he had, he would be worse than a barbarian if he did not respect and honor that friend. God is such a friend. He gives you your breath, He bestows a livelihood upon you, and will you not love Him? You will love your prince if he saves your life, and will you not love God who gives you your life? What magnet is so powerful to draw love as the blessed Deity? He is blind whom beauty does not tempt. He is foolish and senseless who is not drawn with the cords of love. When the body is cold and has no heat in it, it is a sign of death, and that person is dead who has no heat of love in his soul to God. How can he expect love from God, if he shows no love to Him? Will God ever lay such a viper in His chest as casts forth the poison of malice and enmity against Him?

This reproof falls heavy upon the unbelievers of this age, who are so far from loving God that they do all they can to show their hatred of Him. *They declare their sin as Sodom* (Isaiah 3:9). *They set their mouth against the heavens* (Psalm 73:9) in pride and blasphemy, and offer open defiance to God. These are monsters in nature, devils in the shape of men. Let them read their doom: *If any man love not the Lord Jesus Christ, let him be Anathema Maranatha* (1 Corinthians 16:22); that is, let him be accursed from God until Christ's coming to judgment. Let him be heir to a curse while he lives, and at the dreadful day of the Lord, let him hear that heartrending sentence pronounced against him: *Depart from me, ye cursed, into everlasting fire, prepared for the devil and his angels* (Matthew 25:41).

Chapter 5

The Tests of Love for God

Let us test ourselves impartially whether we are in the number of those who love God. To help determine this, as our love will be best seen by the fruits of it, I will provide fourteen signs, or fruits, of love for God, and it concerns us to search carefully whether any of these fruits grow in our garden.

1. The first fruit of love is the contemplation of the mind upon God. He who is in love has his thoughts always upon the object of that love. He who loves God is delighted and captivated with the contemplation of God. *When I awake, I am still with thee* (Psalm 139:18). The thoughts are as travelers in the mind. David's thoughts stayed on the heavenly road: *I am still with thee.* God is the treasure, and where the treasure is, there is the heart. By this we may test our love for God. What are our thoughts most upon? Can we say we are enthralled with delight when we think about God? Do our thoughts have wings? Are they flying upward? Do we contemplate Christ and glory? Oh, how far they are from loving God who hardly ever think of God! *God is not in all his thoughts* (Psalm 10:4). A sinner crowds

God out of his thoughts. He never thinks of God, unless with horror, as the prisoner thinks of the judge.

2. The next fruit of love is desire for communion. Love desires familiarity and fellowship. *My heart and my flesh crieth out for the living God* (Psalm 84:2). King David, being away from the house of God where the tabernacle was, the visible token of His presence, he breathes after God, and in a holy pathos of desire cries out for the living God. Those who love each other desire to be with each other. If we love God, we treasure His ordinances, because there we meet with God. He speaks to us in His Word, and we speak to Him in prayer.

By this let us examine our love for God. Do we desire close communion with God? Those who love each other cannot be away from each other for long. Those who love God have a holy affection; they do not know how to be away from Him. They can bear the lack of anything except God's presence. They can do without health and friends, and they can be happy without a full table, but they cannot be happy without God. *Hide not thy face from me, lest I be like unto them that go down into the pit* (Psalm 143:7). Those who love have their fainting fits. David was ready to faint away and die when he did not have sight of God. Those who love God cannot be content with having ordinances, unless they may enjoy God in them; that would be to lick the glass, and not the honey.

What shall we say to those who can be without God for their entire lives? They think God may be best set aside. They complain that they lack health and business, but not that they lack God! Wicked people are not acquainted with God, and how can they love Him if they do not know Him? What is even worse – they do not desire to be acquainted with Him. *They say unto God, Depart from us; for we desire not the knowledge of thy ways* (Job 21:14). Sinners avoid acquaintance with God.

They consider His presence a burden – and can such people love God? Does that woman love her husband who cannot endure to be in his presence?

3. Another fruit of love is grief. Where there is love for God, there is a grieving for our sins of unkindness against Him. A child who loves his father cannot help but weep for offending him. The heart that burns in love melts in tears. Oh, how dreadful if I should abuse the love of so dear a Savior! Did not my Lord suffer enough upon the cross, but must I make Him suffer more? Will I give Him more gall and vinegar to drink? How disloyal and disingenuous I have been! How I have grieved His Spirit, trampled upon His royal commands, and scorned His blood! This opens a vein of godly sorrow and makes the heart bleed afresh. *Peter . . . went out, and wept bitterly* (Matthew 26:75). When Peter thought about how dearly Christ loved him, about how he was taken up into the Mount of Transfiguration, where Christ showed him the glory of heaven in a vision – it broke his heart with grief that he should deny Christ after he had received such marvelous love from Him. *He went out, and wept bitterly.*

Does a person love his friend who loves to do him harm?

By this let us test our love for God. Do we shed the tears of godly sorrow? Do we grieve because of our unkindness against God, our abuse of mercy, and our lack of improvement of talents? How far they are from loving God who sin daily, and whose hearts never trouble them! They have a sea of sin, and not a drop of sorrow. They are so far from being troubled that they rejoice with their sins. *When thou doest evil, then thou rejoicest* (Jeremiah 11:15). Oh, wretch! Did Christ bleed for sin, and do you laugh at it? Such people are far from loving God. Does a person love his friend who loves to do him harm?

4. Another fruit of love is magnanimity. Love is valiant; it turns cowardice into courage. Love will make one venture upon the greatest difficulties and dangers. The fearful hen will rush upon a dog or serpent to defend her young ones. Love infuses a spirit of gallantry and fortitude into a Christian. He who loves God will stand up in His cause and be a soldier for Him. *We cannot but speak the things which we have seen and heard* (Acts 4:20). He who is afraid to acknowledge Christ has but little love for Him. Nicodemus came sneaking to Christ by night (John 3:2). He was fearful of being seen with Him in the daytime. Love casts out fear (1 John 4:18). As the sun expels fog and mist, so divine love in a great measure expels carnal fear. Does he love God who can hear His blessed truths spoken against and be silent? He who loves his friend will stand up for him, and vindicate him when he is reproached. Does Christ appear for us in heaven, and are we afraid to appear for Him on earth? Love stirs up a Christian; it fires his heart with zeal and strengthens it with courage.

5. The fifth fruit of love is sensitivity. If we love God, our hearts will ache for the dishonor done to God by wicked people. To see not only the banks of the Christian religion, but morality, broken down, and a flood of wickedness coming in; to see God's sabbaths profaned, His oaths violated, and His name dishonored; if there is any love for God in us, we will take these things to heart. Lot's righteous soul was *vexed with the filthy conversation of the wicked* (2 Peter 2:7). The sins of Sodom were as so many spears to pierce his soul. How far are they from loving God who are not at all affected with His dishonor? If they just have peace and business, they take nothing to heart. A man who is dead drunk does not pay attention to or care about someone who may be bleeding to death near him. In the same way, many people who are drunk with the wine of prosperity are

not affected when the honor of God is wounded and His truths lie bleeding. If people love God, they would grieve to see His glory suffer and the Christian religion itself become a martyr.

6. The sixth fruit of love is hatred against sin. Fire purges the impurities from the metal. The fire of love purges out sin. *Ephraim shall say, What have I to do any more with idols?* (Hosea 14:8). He who loves God will have nothing to do with sin, unless to give battle to it. Sin strikes not only at God's honor, but at His being. Does he love his prince who harbors him who is a traitor to the crown? Is he a friend to God who loves that which God hates? The love of God and the love of sin cannot dwell together. The affections cannot be carried to two opposites at the same time. A person cannot love health and love poison too. In the same way, one cannot love God and love sin too. He who allows any secret sin in his heart is as far from loving God as heaven and earth are distant from each other.

7. Another fruit of love is crucifixion. He who loves God is dead to the world. I am crucified to the world (Galatians 6:14). I am dead to its honors and pleasures. He who is in love with God is not much in love with anything else. Love for God and warm love for the world are inconsistent. *If any man love the world, the love of the Father is not in him* (1 John 2:15). Love for God swallows up all other love, just as Aaron's rod swallowed up the Egyptian rods (Exodus 7:12). If a person could live in the sun, what a small point would all the earth be; and when a person's heart is raised above the world in admiring and loving God, how poor and measly are these things below! They seem as nothing in his eye. It was a sign that the early Christians loved God when their property did not lie near their hearts, but they laid down their money at the apostles' feet (Acts 4:35).

Test your love for God by this. What will we think of those

who never have enough of the world? They have the affliction of covetousness, thirsting insatiably after riches. They *pant after the dust of the earth* (Amos 2:7). Ignatius said to never talk of your love for Christ when you prefer the world before the pearl of great price; and are there not many such people who treasure their gold above God? If they have a south land, they do not care for the water of life. They will sell Christ and a good conscience for money. Will God ever bestow heaven upon those who so dishonorably undervalue Him, preferring glittering dust before the glorious Deity? What is there on earth that we should so set our hearts upon it? Only the devil makes us look upon it through a magnifying glass. The world has no real intrinsic worth; it is but paint and deception.

8. The next fruit of love is fear. In those who are godly, love and fear kiss each other. There is a double fear that arises from love.

1. A fear of displeasing. The spouse loves her husband, and therefore will rather deny herself than displease him. The more we love God, the more fearful we are of grieving His Spirit. *How then can I do this great wickedness, and sin against God?* (Genesis 39:9). When Eudoxia, the empress, threatened to banish Chrysostom, he said, "Tell her that I fear nothing but sin." It is a blessed love that puts a Christian into a hot fit of zeal and a cold fit of fear, making him shake and tremble, and not dare to willingly offend God.

2. A fear mixed with jealousy. Eli's heart *trembled for the ark of God* (1 Samuel 4:13). It is not said that his heart trembled for Hophni and Phinehas, his two sons, but that his heart trembled for the ark, because if the ark were taken, then the glory was departed. He who loves God is full of fear lest it should go poorly with the church.

He fears lest profaneness (which is the plague of leprosy) should increase, lest popery gets a foothold, lest God should go from His people. The presence of God in His ordinances is the beauty and strength of a nation. As long as God's presence is with a people, they are safe; but the soul inflamed with love for God fears lest the visible signs of God's presence would be removed.

By this standard, let us test our love for God. Many people fear lest peace and business go away, but not lest God and His gospel go away. Do these people love God? He who loves God is more afraid of the loss of spiritual blessings than physical blessings. If the Sun of righteousness moves out of our horizon, what can follow but darkness? What comfort can an instrument or song give if the gospel is gone? Is it not like the sound of a trumpet or a volley of shot at a funeral?

Many people fear lest peace and business go away, but not lest God and His gospel go away.

9. If we love God, we love what God loves.

1. We love God's Word. David cherished the Word, for the sweetness of it, above honey (Psalm 119:103), and for the value of it, above gold (Psalm 119:72). The lines of Scripture are richer than the mines of gold. Well may we love the Word. It is the guiding star that directs us to heaven. It is the field in which the pearl of great price is hidden. That person who does not love the Word, but thinks it is too strict and could wish any part of the Bible torn out (as an adulterer did in regard to the seventh commandment), has not the least spark of love in his heart.

2. We love God's day. Not only do we keep the Sabbath day, but we love the Sabbath day. *If thou . . . call the sabbath a delight* (Isaiah 58:13). The sabbath is that which keeps up

the regard of religion among us. This day must be consecrated as glorious to the Lord. The house of God is the palace of the great King, and on the sabbath, God shows Himself there *through the lattice* (Song of Solomon 2:9). If we love God, we will treasure His day above all other days. The entire week would be dark if it were not for this day; on this day manna falls double. Now, if ever, heaven's gate stands open, and God comes down in golden mist. On this blessed day, the Sun of righteousness rises upon the soul. A gracious heart treasures that day that was made on purpose for us to enjoy God.

3. We love God's laws. A gracious soul is glad of the law because it restrains his sinful excesses. The heart would be ready to run wild in sin if it did not have some blessed restraints put upon it by the law of God. He who loves God loves His law – the law of repentance, the law of self-denial. Many people say that they love God, but they hate His laws. Let us break their bands asunder and cast away their cords from us (Psalm 2:3). God's precepts are compared to cords; they bind people to their good behavior. However, the wicked think these cords are too tight; therefore they say, "Let us break them." They pretend to love Christ as a Savior, but they hate Him as a King. Christ tells us of His yoke (Matthew 11:29). Sinners would have Christ put a crown upon their head, but not a yoke upon their neck. He would be a strange king who would rule without laws.

4. We love God's picture. We love His image shining in the saints. *Every one that loveth him that begat loveth him also that is begotten of him* (1 John 5:1). It is possible to love a saint, yet not to love him as a saint. We may love him for something else, such as his ingenuity, or because

he is kind and generous. An animal may love a person, but not because he is a person – but because he feeds him and gives him shelter. But to love a saint as he is a saint, this is a sign of love for God. If we love a saint for his saintship, as having something of God in him, then we love him in these four cases:

a. We love a saint, even if he is poor. A person who loves gold loves a piece of gold, even if it is in a rag; and we love a saint, even if he is in rags, because there is something of Christ in him.

b. We love a saint, even if he has many personal failings. There is no perfection here. In some people, impulsive anger prevails; in some people, lack of faithfulness; in others, too much love of the world. A saint in this life is like gold in the ore: much impurity of infirmity clings to him, yet we love him for the grace that is in him. A saint is like a lovely face with a scar: we love the beautiful face of holiness, even though there is a scar in it. The best emerald has its blemishes, the brightest stars have their twinklings, and the best of the saints have their failings. You who cannot love another person because of his infirmities, how could you want God to love you?

c. We love the saints, even though they might differ from us in some lesser things. Perhaps another Christian does not have as much light as you, and that may make him err in some things; will you quickly unsaint him because he cannot come up to your light? Where there is union in fundamentals, there should be union in affections.

d. We love the saints, even though they are persecuted. We love precious metal, even though it is in the furnace. Paul bore in his body *the marks of the Lord Jesus* (Galatians 6:17). Those marks, like the soldier's scars, were honorable. We must love a saint as well in chains as in scarlet. If we love Christ, we love His persecuted members.

If this is love for God, when we love His image sparkling in the saints, then how few people are to be found who truly love God! Do they love God who hate those who are like God? Do they love Christ's person who are filled with a spirit of revenge against His people? How can that wife be said to love her husband who tears his picture? Surely Judas and Julian are not yet dead; their spirit still lives in the world. Who are guilty but the innocent? What greater crime is there than holiness if the devil may be one of the grand jury? Wicked people seem to bear great reverence to the departed saints; they canonize dead saints, but persecute living saints. In vain do men stand up at the creed and tell the world that they believe in God when they disregard one of the articles of the creed – namely, the communion of saints. Surely there is not a greater sign of a person ripe for hell than this – not only to lack grace, but to hate it.

10. Another blessed sign of love is to entertain good thoughts of God. He who loves his friend construes what his friend does in the best sense. Love *thinketh no evil* (1 Corinthians 13:5). Malice interprets everything in the worst sense, but love interprets everything in the best sense. It is an excellent commentator upon providence; it thinks no evil. He who loves God has a good judgment of God; though He afflicts sharply, the soul takes it all well. This is the language of a gracious spirit: "My God sees what a hard heart I have. Therefore, He drives in one wedge of affliction after another, to break my heart. He knows how full I am of bad thoughts and corruption; therefore He brings affliction to purify me and save my life. This severe trial is either to mortify some corruption or to exercise some grace. How good God is to not leave me alone in my sins, but

smites my body to save my soul!" Thus, he who loves God takes everything in stride. Love puts a positive understanding upon all of God's actions. You who are apt to murmur at God as if He had dealt poorly with you, be humbled for this. Say to yourself, "If I loved God more, I would have better thoughts of God." It is Satan who makes us have good thoughts of ourselves and harsh thoughts of God. Love takes everything in the best sense; it thinks no evil.

11. Another fruit of love is obedience. *He that hath my commandments, and keepeth them, he it is that loveth me* (John 14:21). It is a vain thing to say that we love Christ's person if we ignore or disregard His commands. Does that child love his father who refuses to obey him? If we love God, we will obey Him in those things that are contrary to flesh and blood, both (i.) in things difficult and (ii.) in things dangerous.

1. In things difficult – as in shameful sin. There are some sins that are not only as near to us as the garment, but are as dear to us as the eye. If we love God, we will set ourselves against these, both in purpose and practice. Another difficult thing is to forgive our enemies. God commands us upon pain of death to forgive. Forgive one another (Ephesians 4:32). This is difficult. It is crossing the stream. We tend to forget kindnesses and remember harm; but if we love God, we will overlook injustices. When we seriously consider how many times God has forgiven us, how many insults and provocations He has put up with at our hands, this makes us follow His Word and endeavor to bury an injustice rather than to avenge it.

We tend to forget kindnesses and remember harm; but if we love God, we will overlook injustices.

2. In things dangerous. When God calls us to suffer for Him, we will obey. Love made Christ suffer for us. Love was the chain that fastened Him to the cross. So if we love God, we will be willing to suffer for Him. Love has a strange quality: it is the least suffering grace, yet it is the most suffering grace. It is the least tolerant grace in one sense. It will not allow known sin to lie in the soul unrepented of, and it will not tolerate abuses and dishonors done to God; thus it is the least tolerant grace. Yet it is also the most tolerant grace. It will endure reproaches, chains, and imprisonments for Christ's sake. *I am ready not to be bound only, but also to die . . . for the name of the Lord Jesus* (Acts 21:13). It is true that every Christian is not a martyr, but he has the spirit of martyrdom in him. He says with Paul, "I am ready to be bound." He has a disposition of mind to suffer, if God calls him to do so. Love will carry people out above their own strength.

Tertullian observed how much the heathen suffered for love for their country. If the fountainhead of nature rises so high, surely grace will rise higher. If love for their country will make people suffer, much more should love for Christ. Love *endureth all things* (1 Corinthians 13:7). Basil spoke of a young woman condemned to the fire who had her life and possessions offered to her if she would fall down to the idol. She answered, "Let life and money go; welcome Christ." It was a noble and zealous speech of Ignatius when he said, "Let me be ground with the teeth of wild beasts if I may be God's pure wheat." How divine affection carried the early saints above the love of life and the fear of death! Stephen was stoned, Luke was hanged on an olive tree, and Peter was crucified at Jerusalem with his head downward. These divine heroes were willing to suffer rather than to make the name of God suffer by their cowardice. How Paul treasured his chains that he wore for Christ! He gloried in it as a woman who is proud of her jewels, said Chrysostom. And holy Ignatius wore his chains as a bracelet of diamonds, *not accepting deliverance* (Hebrews 11:35). They refused to come out of prison on sinful terms. They preferred their innocence before their liberty.

By this let us test our love for God. Do we have the spirit of martyrdom? Many people say that they love God, but how does it appear? They will not give up the least comfort, or pick up the least cross, for His sake. If Jesus Christ would have said to us, "I love you much. You are dear to Me, but I cannot suffer or lay down My life for you," we would have questioned His love very much; and may not Christ suspect us when we pretend to love Him, yet will endure nothing for Him?

He who loves God will try to make Him appear glorious in the eyes of others.

12. He who loves God will try to make Him appear glorious in the eyes of others. Those who are in love will be commending and setting forth the graciousness of those people whom they love. If we love God, we will spread abroad His excellencies so that we may raise His fame and esteem, and may persuade others to fall in love with Him. Love cannot be silent. We will be as trumpets sounding forth the freeness of God's grace, the transcendence of His love, and the glory of His kingdom. Love is like fire: where it burns in the heart, it will break forth at the lips. It will be elegant in setting forth God's praise; love must have vent.

13. Another fruit of love is to long for Christ's appearing. *Henceforth there is laid up for me a crown of righteousness, . . . and not to me only, but unto all them also that love his appearing* (2 Timothy 4:8). Love desires union. Aristotle gives the reason that it is because joy flows upon union. When our union with

Christ is perfect in glory, then our joy will be full. He who loves Christ loves His appearing. Christ's appearing will be a happy appearing to the saints. His appearing now is very comforting when He appears for us as an advocate (Hebrews 9:24), but the other appearing will be infinitely more so, when He will appear for us as our Husband. He will at that day bestow two jewels upon us: His love – a love so great and astonishing that it is better felt than expressed; and His likeness. *When he shall appear, we shall be like him* (1 John 3:2). And from both of these, love and likeness, infinite joy will flow into the soul. It is no wonder, then, that he who loves Christ longs for His appearance. *The Spirit and the bride say come. . . . Even so, come, Lord Jesus* (Revelation 22:17, 20). By this, let us test our love for Christ. A wicked person who is self-condemned is afraid of Christ's appearing, and wishes He would never appear; but those who love Christ are joyful to think of His coming in the clouds. They will then be delivered from all their sins and fears, they will be acquitted before men and angels, and they will be forever transported into the paradise of God.

14. Love will make us willing to perform the lowest duties. Love is a humble grace. It does not walk around in superiority, but will crawl upon its hands and knees. It will lower itself and submit to anything whereby it may be serviceable to Christ. As we see in Joseph of Arimathea and Nicodemus, both of them honorable people, yet one takes down Christ's body with his own hands, and the other embalms it with sweet fragrances. It might seem much for people of their rank to be employed in that service, but love made them do it. If we love God, we will not think that any work is too low for us by which we may be helpful to Christ's members. Love is not squeamish. It will visit the sick, relieve the poor, and wash the saints' wounds. The mother who loves her child is not reluctant and restrained;

she will do those things for her child that others would hate to do. He who loves God will humble himself to the lowest office of love for Christ and His members.

These are the fruits of love for God. Happy are they who can find these fruits, so foreign to their natures, growing in their souls.

Chapter 6

An Exhortation to Love God

1. An exhortation to love God.

Let me earnestly urge all who bear the name of Christians to learn to truly love God. *O love the LORD, all ye his saints* (Psalm 31:23). There are not many who love God. Many people give Him hypocritical kisses, but few love Him. It is not as easy to love God as most people imagine. The affection of love is natural, but the grace is not. By nature, people are haters of God (Romans 1:30). The wicked want to flee from God. They neither want to be under His rules nor within His reach. They fear God, but do not love Him. All the strength in men or angels cannot make the heart love God. Ordinances will not do it of themselves, nor judgments; only the almighty and invincible power of the Spirit of God can infuse love into the soul. Since this is such a difficult thing, it calls upon us for more earnest prayer and effort after this angelic grace of love. To inspire and inflame our desires after it, I will provide twenty motives for loving God.

1. Without this, all our religion is vain. It is not duty, but love for our duty that God looks at. It is not how much we do, but how much we love. If a servant does not do his work willingly and out of love, it is not acceptable. Duties that are not mingled

with love are as burdensome to God as they are to us. David therefore counsels his son Solomon to serve God with a *willing mind* (1 Chronicles 28:9). To do our duty without love is not sacrifice, but penance.

2. Love is the most noble and excellent grace. It is a pure flame kindled from heaven. By it we resemble God, who is love. Believing and obeying do not make us like God, but by love we grow like Him (1 John 4:16). Love is a grace that most delights in God, and is most delightful to Him. That disciple who was most full of love lay on Christ's chest. Love puts a vigor and luster upon all the graces. The graces seem to be eclipsed unless love shines and sparkles in them. Faith is not true unless it works by love. The waters of repentance are not pure unless they flow from the spring of love. Love is the incense that makes all our services fragrant and acceptable to God.

3. Is that which God requires unreasonable? It is simply our love. If He would ask for our possessions or our children, could we deny Him? But He asks only for our love. He would only pick this flower. Is this a difficult request? Was there ever any debt as easily paid as this? We do not at all impoverish ourselves by paying it. Love is not a burden. Is it any labor for the bride to love her husband? Love is delightful.

4. God is the most adequate and complete object of our love. All the excellencies that lie scattered in the creatures are united in Him. He is wisdom, beauty, and love. Yes, He is the very essence of goodness. There is nothing in God that can cause us to hate Him. The creature sooner overindulges than satisfies, but there are fresh delights sparkling forth in God. The more we enjoy of Him, the more we are ravished with delight.

There is nothing in God to deaden our affections or quench

our love. There is no weakness or flaw such as usually weaken and cool love. There is that excellence in God that may not only invite, but command our love. If there were more angels in heaven than there are, and all those glorious seraphim had an immense flame of love burning in their hearts to eternity, yet they could not love God equivalently to that infinite perfection and transcendence of goodness that is in Him. Surely, then, this is enough to persuade us to love God. We cannot spend our love upon a better object.

5. Love advances true religion. It oils the wheels of the affections and makes them more active and cheerful in God's service. Love takes off the tediousness of duty. Jacob thought seven years but little for the love he had for Rachel. Love makes duty a pleasure. Why are the angels *He who loves God is never weary of telling it.* so swift and winged in God's service? It is because they love Him. Love is never weary. He who loves God is never weary of telling it. He who loves God is never weary of serving Him.

6. God desires our love. We have lost our beauty and stained our blood, yet the King of heaven desires our love. What is there in our love that God should seek it? How does God benefit from our love? He does not need it. He is infinitely blessed in Himself. If we deny Him our love, He has more sublime creatures who pay the cheerful tribute of love to Him. God does not need our love, yet He seeks it.

7. God has deserved our love; how He has loved us! Our affections should be kindled at the fire of God's love. What a miracle of love it is that God would love us when there was nothing lovely in us! *I said unto thee when thou wast in thy blood, Live* (Ezekiel 16:6). The time of our loathing was the time of God's

loving. We had something in us to provoke fury, but nothing to excite love. What love, passing understanding, was it to give Christ to us – that Christ would die for sinners! God has set all the angels in heaven wondering at this love. Augustine said, "The cross is a pulpit, and the lesson Christ preached on it is love." Oh, the living love of a dying Savior! I think I see Christ upon the cross bleeding all over! I think I hear Him say to us, "Reach out your hands to Me. Put them into My sides. Feel My bleeding heart. See if I do not love you. And will you not bestow your love upon Me? Will you love the world more than Me? Did the world appease the wrath of God for you? Have I not done all this? And will you not love Me?" It is natural to love when we are loved. Christ has given to us an example of love, and has written it with His blood. Let us labor to follow such an example and to imitate Him in love.

8. Love for God is the best self-love. It is self-love to get the soul saved. By loving God, we forward our own salvation. *He that dwelleth in love dwelleth in God, and God in him* (1 John 4:16). He who has God dwelling in his heart is sure to dwell with God in heaven. So to love God is the truest self-love. He who does not love God does not love himself.

9. Love for God demonstrates sincerity. *The upright love thee* (Song of Solomon 1:4). Many children of God fear that they are hypocrites. Do you love God? When Peter was dejected with the sense of his sin, he thought himself unworthy that Christ would ever take notice of him or use him more in the work of his apostleship. See, though, how Christ went about to comfort him. *Simon, son of Jonas, lovest thou me?* (John 21:15). It is as if Christ had said, "Although you denied Me through fear, yet if you can say from your heart that you love Me, you are sincere and upright."

To love God is a better sign of sincerity than to fear Him. The Israelites feared God's justice. *When he slew them, then they sought him; and they returned and enquired early after God* (Psalm 78:34). But what did all this come to? *Nevertheless they did flatter him with their mouth, and they lied unto him with their tongues. For their heart was not right with him* (Psalm 78:36-37). That repentance that comes only from fear of God's judgments is no better than flattery, and has no love mixed with it. Loving God demonstrates that God has the heart; and if the heart is His, that will direct all the rest.

10. By our love for God, we may conclude God's love for us. *We love him, because he first loved us* (1 John 4:19). Oh, says the soul, if I knew that God loved me, I could rejoice! Do you love God? Then you may be sure of God's love for you. As it is with magnifying glasses, if the glass gets hot and causes a burn, it is because the sun has first shined upon it, or else it could not burn. In the same way, if our hearts burn in love for God, it is because God's love has first shined upon us, or else we could not burn in love. Our love is nothing but the reflection of God's love.

11. If you do not love God, you will love something else – either the world or sin; and are those worthy of your love? Is it not better to love God than these? It is better to love God than the world, as appears in the following points.

If you set your love on worldly things, they will not satisfy. You may as well satisfy your body with air as your soul with earth. *In the fullness of his sufficiency he shall be in straits* (Job 20:22). Abundance has its deficiency. Even if you had all of the world, it would not fill your soul. And will you set your love on that which will never give you contentment? Is it not better to love God? He will give you that which will satisfy. *I shall be satisfied, when I awake, with thy likeness* (Psalm 17:15). When I awake out of the sleep of death, and will have some of the rays and beams of God's glory put upon me, I will then be satisfied with His likeness.

If you love worldly things, they cannot remove trouble of mind. If there is a thorn in the conscience, all the world cannot remove it. King Saul was troubled in mind, and all his crown jewels could not comfort him (1 Samuel 28:15). But if you love God, He can give you peace when nothing else can. He can turn *the shadow of death into the morning* (Amos 5:8). He can apply Christ's blood to refresh your soul. He can whisper His love by the Spirit, and with one smile scatter all your fears and worries.

If you love the world, you love that which may keep you out of heaven. Worldly contentment may be compared to the wagons in an army; while the soldiers have been supplying themselves at the wagons, they have lost the battle. *How hardly shall they that have riches enter into the kingdom of God!* (Mark 10:23). To many people, prosperity is like the sail to the boat, which quickly overturns it; so that by loving the world, you love that which will endanger you. But if you love God, there is no fear of losing heaven. He will be a Rock to hide you, but not to hurt you. By loving Him, we come to enjoy Him.

You may love worldly things, but they cannot love you in return. You love gold and silver, but your gold cannot love you in return. You love a picture, but the picture cannot love you in return. You give away your love to the creature, and receive no love back. But if you love God, He will love you in return. *If a man love me, he will keep my words: and my Father will love him, and we will come unto him, and make our abode with him* (John 14:23). God will not be behind in love to us; for our drop, we will receive an ocean.

When you love the world, you love that which is worse than yourselves. The soul, as John of Damascus said, is a sparkle of celestial brightness; it carries in it an idea and resemblance of God. While you love the world, you love that which is infinitely below the worth of your souls. Will anyone pay lavishly for sackcloth? When you give your love to the world, you hang a pearl upon a swine; you love that which is inferior to yourself. As Christ speaks in another sense of the birds of the air, *Are ye not much better than they?* (Matthew 6:26), so I say of worldly things, "Are you not much better than they?" You love a nice house or a beautiful picture; are you not much better than they? But if you love God, you place your love on the most noble and sublime object; you love that which is better than yourselves. God is better than the soul, better than angels, and better than heaven.

You may love the world and have hatred for your love. *Because ye are not of the world, . . . therefore the world hateth you* (John 15:19). Would it not upset someone to spend money upon a piece of land that, instead of bringing forth corn or grapes, would yield nothing but thorns and weeds? That is how it is with all worldly things. We love them, and they prove to be nothing but stinging nettles. We meet with nothing but disappointment. *Let fire come out of the bramble, and devour the cedars of Lebanon* (Judges 9:15). While we love the creature, fire comes out of this bramble to devour us; but if we love God, He will not return hatred for love. *I love them that love me* (Proverbs 8:17). God may chastise, but He cannot hate. Every believer is part of Christ, and God can as well hate Christ as hate a believer.

You may overlove the creature. You may love wine too much and silver too much, but you cannot love God too much. If it were possible to exceed, then excess in this would be a virtue; but it is our sin that we cannot love God enough. *How weak is thine heart* (Ezekiel 16:30). So it may be said, How weak is our love for God! If we could love God far more than we do, yet it still would not be proportionate to His worth. There is no danger of excess in our love for God.

You may love worldly things, and they die and leave you. Riches take wings, and relatives drop away. There is nothing here abiding. The creature has a little honey in its mouth, but it has wings; it will soon fly away. But if you love God, He is a *portion for ever* (Psalm 73:26). He is called a Sun for comfort, and a Rock for eternity; He abides forever. Thus we see it is better to love God than to love the world.

If it is better to love God than to love the world, then surely it is also better to love God than to love sin. What is there in sin that anyone would love it? Sin is a debt. *Forgive us our debts* (Matthew 6:12). It is a debt that gives us over to the wrath of God; why would we love sin? Does anyone love to be in debt? Sin is a disease. *The whole head is sick* (Isaiah 1:5). And will you love sin? Will any person embrace a disease? Will he love his plague sores? Sin is a pollution. The apostle James calls it *filthiness* (James 1:21). It is compared to leprosy and to poison of asps. God's heart rises against sinners. *My soul loathed them* (Zechariah 11:8). Sin is a deformed monster. Lust makes a person like a beast; malice makes him devilish. What is in sin to be loved? Will we love deformity? Sin is an enemy. It is compared to a *serpent* (Proverbs 23:32). It has four stings: shame, guilt, horror, and death. Will a person love that which seeks his death? Surely, then, it is better to love God than to love sin. God will save you; sin will damn you. Has he not become foolish who loves damnation?

12. The relationship we stand in with God calls for love. It is a close relationship. *Thy Maker is thine husband* (Isaiah 54:5). And will a wife not love her husband? He is full of tenderness. His spouse is to Him as the apple of His eye (Zechariah 2:8).

He rejoices over her as the bridegroom rejoices over the bride (Isaiah 52:5). He loves the believer as He loves Christ (John 17:26). The same love for quality, though not equally. Either we must love God, or we give reason for suspicion that we are not yet united to Him.

13. Love is the most abiding grace. This will stay with us when other graces take their farewell. In heaven we will need no repentance because we will have no sin. In heaven we will not need patience because there will be no affliction. In heaven we will need no faith because faith looks at things unseen (Hebrews 11:1). But then we will see God face-to-face, and where there is vision, there is no need of faith.

But when the other graces are out of date, love continues; and in this sense the apostle Paul says that love is greater than faith because it abides the longest. *Charity never faileth* (1 Corinthians 13:8). Faith is the staff we walk with in this life. *We walk by faith* (2 Corinthians 5:7). But we will leave this staff at heaven's door, and only love will enter. Thus love carries away the crown from all the other graces. Love is the most long-lived grace. It is a blossom of eternity. How we should strive to excel in this grace, which alone will live with us in heaven, and will accompany us to the marriage supper of the Lamb!

14. Love for God will never let sin thrive in the heart. Some plants will not thrive when they are close together. The love of God withers sin. Though the old nature lives, it is as a sick man; it is weak and draws its breath short. The flower of love kills the weed of sin. Although sin does not die perfectly, yet it dies daily. How we should labor for that grace that is the only thing to destroy sin!

15. Love for God is an excellent means for growth of grace. *But*

grow in grace (2 Peter 3:18). Growth in grace is very pleasing to God. Christ accepts the truth of grace, but commends the degrees of grace; and what can more promote and enhance grace than love for God? Love is like watering the root, which makes the tree grow. Therefore the apostle Paul uses this expression in his prayer: *The Lord direct your hearts into the love of God* (2 Thessalonians 3:5). He knew that this grace of love would nurse and cherish all the graces.

16. Great benefit to us will result if we love God. *Eye hath not seen, nor ear heard, neither have entered into the heart of man, the things which God hath prepared for them that love him* (1 Corinthians 2:9). The eye has seen rare sights, and the ear has heard sweet music; but eye has not seen, nor ear heard, nor can the heart of man conceive what God has prepared for those who love Him! As Augustine said, such glorious rewards are laid up that faith itself is not able to comprehend. God has promised a crown of life to those who love Him (James 1:12). This crown encircles within it all blessedness – riches, glory, and delight; and it is a crown that does not fade away (1 Peter 5:4). Thus God would draw us to Him by rewards.

17. Love for God is tested and proven armor against error. For lack of hearts full of love, people have heads full of error. Unholy opinions are a result of a lack of holy affections. Why are people given up to strong delusions? *Because they received not the love of the truth* (2 Thessalonians 2:10-11). The more we love God, the more we hate those freethinking opinions that would take us away from God and into depravity and sin.

18. If we love God, we have all winds blowing for us; everything in the world will conspire for our good. We do not know what fiery trials we may meet with, but to those who love God, all

things will work for good. Those things that work against them will work for them. Their cross will make way for a crown. Every wind will blow them to the heavenly port.

19. Lack of love for God is the foundation of apostasy. The seed in the parable that had no root withered away (Matthew 13:6). He who does not have the love of God rooted in his heart will fall away in time of temptation. He who loves God will cling to Him, as Ruth did to Naomi. *Whither thou goest, I will go; and where thou lodgest, I will lodge: thy people shall be my people, and thy God my God: where thou diest, will I die* (Ruth 1:16-17). However, he who lacks love for God will do as Orpah did to her mother-in-law: she kissed her and took her farewell of her. You can consider that person an apostate who has no love in his heart for God.

Lack of love for God is the foundation of apostasy.

20. Love is the only thing in which we can retaliate with God. If God is angry with us, we must not be angry at Him in return. If He rebukes us, we must not rebuke Him in return. However, if God loves us, we must love Him in return. There is nothing in which we can answer God in return except for love. We must not give Him word for word, but we must give Him love for love.

Thus we have seen twenty motives to inspire and inflame our love for God.

Question: What will we do to love God?

Answer: Study God. If we studied Him more, we would love Him more. Take a view of His superlative greatness, His holiness, and His incomprehensible goodness. The angels know God better than we do, and they clearly behold the splendor of His majesty; therefore, they are so deeply enamored with Him.

Labor for an interest in God. *O God, thou art my God* (Psalm 63:1). That pronoun "my" is a sweet attraction to love; a person loves that which is his own. The more we believe, the more we love. Faith is the root, and love is the flower that grows upon it. *Faith which worketh by love* (Galatians 5:6).

Make it your earnest request to God that He will give you a heart to love Him. This is an acceptable request, and surely God will not deny it. When King Solomon asked for wisdom from God – *Give therefore thy servant an understanding heart – the speech pleased the LORD* (1 Kings 3:9-10). So when you cry to God, "Lord, give me a heart to love You. It is my anguish that I do not love You more. Oh, kindle this fire from heaven upon the altar of my heart!" – surely this prayer pleases the Lord, and He will pour His Spirit upon you, whose golden oil will make the lamp of your love burn bright.

2. An exhortation to preserve your love for God.

You who have love for God, strive to preserve it. Do not let this love die and be quenched. As you desire God's love to be continued to you, so let your love be continued to Him. Love, as fire, will be ready to go out. *Thou hast left thy first love* (Revelation 2:4). Satan labors to blow out this flame, and through neglect of duty we lose it. When a frail body takes off layers of clothing, it is apt to get cold; and when we leave off duty, by degrees we cool in our love for God. Of all graces, love is most likely to decay; therefore, we need to be more careful to preserve it. If a man has a jewel, he will keep it. If he has land of inheritance, he will keep it. What care, then, should we have to keep this grace of love! It is sad to see professing Christians declining in their love for God. Many are in a spiritual decline; their love is decaying.

There are four signs by which Christians may know that their love is decaying.

1. When they have lost their taste. He who is in a deep consumption has no taste; he does not find that savory delight in his food as formerly. So when Christians have lost their taste, and they find no sweetness in a promise, it is a sign of a spiritual consumption. *If so be ye have tasted that the Lord is gracious* (1 Peter 2:3). There was a time when they found comfort in drawing near to God. His Word was as the dripping honey, very delicious to the palate of their soul; but now it is otherwise. They can taste no more sweetness in spiritual things than *in the white of an egg* (Job 6:6). This is a sign that they are in decay. To lose the taste argues for the loss of the first love.

2. When Christians have lost their appetite. A person in a deep consumption does not have that delight for his food as formerly. There was a time when Christians did *hunger and thirst after righteousness* (Matthew 5:6). They cared about things of a heavenly aspect, such as the grace of the Spirit, the blood of the cross, and the light of God's countenance. They had a longing for ordinances, and came to them as a hungry man to a feast. But now the case is different. They have no appetite; they do not so treasure Christ. They do not have such strong affections for the Word, and their hearts do not burn within them. This is a sad sign. They are in a consumption, and their love is decaying. It was a sign that David's natural strength was decreasing when they covered him with clothes, yet he could not get warm (1 Kings 1:1). So when men are piled with hot clothes (or ordinances), yet they have no heat of affection, but are cold and stiff, as if they were ready to be

laid forth – this is a sign that their first love has declined and that they are in a deep consumption, or decay.

3. When Christians grow more in love with the world, it declares the decrease of spiritual love. They were once of a splendid, heavenly character. They spoke the language of Canaan. Now, though, they are like the fish in the gospel that had money in its mouth (Matthew 17:27). They cannot speak three words without one of them being about the world. Their thoughts and affections, like Satan, are still compassing the earth – a sign that they are going downhill quickly and that their love for God is in decline. We can observe that when nature decays and grows weaker, people walk bent over more; and truly, when the heart goes more bent to the earth, and is so bowed over that it can scarcely lift up itself to a heavenly thought, it is now sadly declining in its first love. When rust clings to metal, it not only takes away the brightness of the metal, but it corrodes and consumes it. And when the world clings to people's souls, it not only hinders the shining luster of their graces, but by degrees it corrodes them.

4. When Christians give little consideration to God's worship. Duties of religion are performed in a dead, formal manner. If they are not left undone, yet they are poorly done. This is a sad symptom of spiritual decay. Carelessness in duty shows a decay in our first love. The violin can never make good music if its strings are loose. When people grow slack in duty, they pray as if they prayed not. This can never make any harmonious sound in God's ears. When the spiritual motion is slow and heavy, and the pulse of the soul beats low, it is a sign that Christians have left their first love.

Let us take heed of this spiritual decay. It is dangerous to fall away in our love. Love is such a grace that we do not know how to be without it. A soldier may as well be without his weapons, an artist without his pencil, or a musician without his instrument as a Christian can be without love. The body cannot lack its natural heat. Love is to the soul as the natural heat is to the body; there is no life without it. Love influences the graces, it excites the affections, it makes us grieve for sin, and it makes us cheerful in God. It is like oil to the wheels. It strengthens us in God's service. How careful, then, we should be to keep alive our love for God!

Question: How may we keep our love from going out?

Answer: Watch your hearts every day. Take notice of the first dwindlings in grace. Observe yourselves when you begin to grow lifeless and indifferent, and use all means for being strengthened and enlivened. Be much in prayer, meditation, and holy discussion. When the fire is going out, you throw on fuel; and when the flame of your love is going out, make use of ordinances and gospel promises as fuel to keep the fire of your love burning.

> *Love is to the soul as the natural heat is to the body; there is no life without it.*

3. An exhortation to increase your love for God.

Let me exhort Christians to increase your love for God. Let your love be raised up higher. *And this I pray, that your love may abound yet more and more* (Philippians 1:9). Our love for God should be as the light of the morning: first there is the daybreak, and then it shines brighter to the full meridian. Those who have a few sparks of love should stir up those divine sparks into a flame. A Christian should not be content with so small a bit of grace as may make him wonder whether he has any grace or not, but should be still increasing the supply. He who has a little gold wants more. You who love God a little, strive to love Him more. A godly person is content with very little of the world, yet he is never satisfied. He always desires more of the Spirit's influence, and labors to add one degree of love to another. To persuade Christians to put more oil to the lamp and increase the flame of their love, let me propose these four divine incentives:

1. The growth of love displays its truth. If I see the almond tree bud and flourish, I know that there is life in the root. Paint will not grow; a hypocrite, who is but a picture, will not grow. But where we see love for God increasing and growing larger, as Elijah's cloud, we may conclude that it is true and genuine.

2. By the growth of love, we imitate the saints in the Bible. Their love for God, like the waters of the sanctuary, rose higher (Ezekiel 47). The disciples' love for Christ at first was weak; they fled from Christ. But after Christ's death, it grew more vigorous, and they made an open profession of Him. Peter's love at first was more wavering and weak; he denied Christ. But afterward, how boldly he preached Him! When Christ put him to a trial of his love – *Simon, son of Jonas, lovest thou Me?* (John 21:16) – Peter could make his humble yet confident appeal to Christ: *Yea, Lord; thou knowest that I love thee.* Thus that tender plant that before was blown down with the wind of a temptation has now grown into a cedar, which all the powers of hell cannot shake.

3. The growth of love will amplify the reward. The more we burn in love, the more we will shine in glory. The higher our love, the brighter our crown.

4. The more we love God, the more love we will have from Him. Do we want God to reveal the sweet secrets of His love to us? Do we want the smiles of His face? Oh, then let us strive for higher degrees of love. Paul considered gold and pearls as mere dung in comparison to Christ (Philippians 3:8). Yes, he was so inflamed with love for God that he could have wished himself accursed from Christ for his brethren, the Jews (Romans 9:3). It is not that he could be accursed from Christ, but such was his fervent love and pious zeal for the glory of God that he would have been content to have suffered, even beyond what is fit to speak, if God might have had more honor.

Here was love stretched to the highest pitch that it was possible for a human to arrive at, and behold, how near he lay to God's heart! The Lord took him up to heaven awhile, and laid him in His arms, where he had such a glorious sight of God, and heard those *unspeakable words, which it is not lawful for a man to utter* (2 Corinthians 12:4). No one ever lost by his love for God.

If our love for God does not increase, it will soon decrease. If the fire is not blown up, it will quickly go out. Therefore, Christians should above all things endeavor to cherish and strengthen their love for God. This exhortation will be out of date when we get to heaven, for then our light will be clear and our love perfect; but now it is in season to exhort so that our love for God may abound yet more and more.

Chapter 7

Effectual Calling

The second qualification of the people to whom this privilege in the text belongs is that they are the called of God. All things work for good *to them who are the called* (Romans 8:28). Though this word "called" is placed in order after loving God, yet in nature it goes before it. Love is first named, but not first worked; we must be called by God before we can love God.

Calling is made the middle link of the golden chain of salvation (Romans 8:30). It is placed between predestination and glorification; and if we have this middle link secured, we are sure of the two other ends of the chain. To more clearly illustrate this, let us observe six things.

1. A distinction about calling. There is a twofold call.

1. There is an outward call, which is nothing else but God's blessed offer of grace in the gospel, His communicating with sinners, when He invites them to come in and accept His mercy. Our Savior speaks about this when He says, *Many be called, but few chosen* (Matthew 20:16). This external call is insufficient for salvation, yet it is sufficient to leave people without excuse.

2. There is an inward call, when God wonderfully overpowers the heart and draws the will to embrace Christ. Augustine calls this an effectual call. God, by the outward call, blows a trumpet in the ear; by the inward call, He opens the heart, as He did with the heart of Lydia (Acts 16:14). The outward call may bring people to a profession of Christ, but the inward call brings them to a possession of Christ. The outward call restrains a sinner, but the inward call changes him.

2. Our deplorable condition before we are called.

1. We are in a state of enslavement. Before God calls a person, he is at the devil's call. If he says, "Go," he goes. The foolish sinner is like the slave who digs in the mine, hews in the quarry, or tugs at the oar. He is at the command of Satan, as the donkey is at the command of the driver.

2. We are in a state of darkness. *Ye were sometimes darkness* (Ephesians 5:8). Darkness is very dismal. A person in the dark is full of fear. He trembles with every step he takes. Darkness is dangerous. He who is in the dark may quickly go out of the right way and fall into rivers or whirlpools, and in the darkness of ignorance, we may quickly fall into the whirlpool of hell.

3. We are in a state of weakness. *When we were yet without strength* (Romans 5:6). We had no strength to resist a temptation or fight with a corruption. Sin cut the lock of hair in which our strength lay (Judges 16:20). There is not only weakness, but there is also stubbornness. *Ye do always resist the Holy Ghost* (Acts 7:51). In addition to resistance to good, there is opposition.

4. We are in a state of pollution. *I . . . saw thee polluted in*

thine own blood (Ezekiel 16:6). The imagination formulates worldly thoughts. The heart is the devil's forge, where the sparks of lust fly.

5. We are in a state of damnation. We are born under a curse. The wrath of God abides on us (John 3:36). This is our condition before God sees fit by a merciful call to bring us near to Himself and free us from that misery in which we were before engulfed.

3. The means of our effectual call. The typical means that the Lord uses in calling us is not by visions and revelations, but by His Word and His Spirit.

1. By His Word, which is the rod of His strength (Psalm 110:2). The voice of the Word is God's call to us. Therefore He is said to speak to us from heaven (Hebrews 12:25) – that is, in the ministry of the Word. When the Word calls us from sin, it is as if we heard a voice from heaven.

2. By His Spirit. This is the loud call. The Word is the practical cause of our conversion, and the Spirit is the powerful cause. The ministers of God are only the pipes and organs. It is the Spirit blowing in them that effectually changes the heart. *While Peter yet spake these words, the Holy Ghost fell on all them which heard the word* (Acts 10:44). The farmer's hard work in plowing and sowing will not make the ground productive without the early and latter rain. In the same way, it is not the seed of the Word that will effectually convert the heart unless the Spirit puts forth His pleasing influence and drops as rain upon the heart. Therefore, the aid of God's Spirit is to be sought, that He would put forth His powerful voice and awaken us out of the grave of unbelief. If a man knocks at a gate of brass, it will not open; but if he comes with a key in

his hand, it will open. And when God, who has the key of David in His hand (Revelation 3:7), comes, He opens the heart, even if it is firmly locked against Him.

4. The method God uses in calling sinners. The Lord does not limit Himself to one particular way or use the same method with all. He comes sometimes in a still, small voice. Those who have had godly parents, and have sat under the warm sunshine of Christian education, often do not know how or when they were called. The Lord quietly and gradually instilled grace into their hearts, as the dew falls unnoticed in drops. They know by the heavenly effects that they are called, but they do not know the time or manner. The hand moves on the clock, but they do not perceive when it moves. That is how God deals with some people.

Others are more stubborn and difficult sinners, and God comes to them in a rough wind. He uses more wedges of the law to break their hearts. He deeply humbles them and shows them that they are damned without Christ. Then, having plowed up the fallow ground of their hearts by humbling them, He sows the seed of consolation. He presents Christ and mercy to them and draws their wills, not only to accept Christ, but passionately to desire and faithfully to rest upon Him. That is how He worked upon Paul and called him from a persecutor to a preacher. This call, although it is more visible than the other, yet it is not more real. God's method in calling sinners may vary, but the effect is still the same.

5. The properties of this effectual calling.

1. It is a sweet call. God calls us as He allures. He does not force us, but draws us to Him. The freedom of the will is not taken away, but the stubbornness of it is

conquered. *Thy people shall be willing in the day of thy power* (Psalm 110:3). After this call, there are no more disputes. The soul willingly obeys God's call – as when Christ called Zacchaeus, who then joyfully welcomed Him into his heart and house.

2. It is a holy call. He has *called us with an holy calling* (2 Timothy 1:9). This call of God calls people out of their sins. By this calling, they are consecrated and set apart for God. The vessels of the tabernacle were taken from common use and set apart to a holy use. In the same way, those who are genuinely called are separated from sin and consecrated to God's service. The God whom we worship is holy, the work we are employed in is holy, and the place we hope to arrive at is holy; all this calls for holiness. A Christian's heart is to be the welcoming room of the blessed Trinity; and should not *holiness to the* LORD be written upon it (Exodus 28:36; Zechariah 14:20-21)? Believers are children of God the Father, members of God the Son, and temples of God the Holy Spirit – and will they not be holy? Holiness is the badge and uniform of God's people: *The people of thy holiness* (Isaiah 63:18).

Just as chastity distinguishes a virtuous woman from a harlot, so holiness distinguishes the godly from the wicked. It is a holy calling. *For God hath not called us unto uncleanness, but unto holiness* (1 Thessalonians 4:7). Do not let anyone who lives in sin say that he is called of God. Has God called you to be a swearer or a drunkard? No; do not let the merely moral person say that he is effectually called. What is civility without sanctity? It is merely a dead carcass covered with flowers. The king's picture stamped upon brass will not be accepted as gold. The merely moral man looks as if he had the King of heaven's image stamped upon him, but he is no better than counterfeit metal, which will not pass for currency with God.

3. It is an irresistible call. When God calls someone by His grace, he cannot help but come. You may resist the minister's call, but you cannot resist the Spirit's call. The finger of the blessed Spirit can write upon a heart of stone, just as He once wrote His laws upon tablets of stone. God's words are creating words. When He said, *Let there be light*, then *there was light* (Genesis 1:3); and when He says, "Let there be faith," it shall be so. When God called Paul, he answered to the call: *I was not disobedient unto the heavenly vision* (Acts 26:19). God rides forth conquering in the chariot of His gospel. He makes the blind eyes see and the stony heart bleed.

If God will call someone, nothing will lie in the way to hinder. Difficulties will be removed, and the powers of hell will be scattered. *Who hath resisted his will?* (Romans 9:19). God bends the bars of iron sinew and cuts apart the gates of brass (Psalm 107:16). When the Lord touches a person's heart by His Spirit, all vain thoughts are brought down, and the great fort of the will yields to God. I may allude to Psalm 114: 5: *What ailed thee, O thou sea, that thou fleddest? Thou Jordan, that thou wert driven back?* The person who before was as a raging sea, foaming forth wickedness, now suddenly falls back and trembles. He falls down as the jailer and asks, *What must I do to be saved?* (Acts 16:30). What worries you, O sea? What disturbs this person? The Lord has been effectually calling him. He has been working a work of grace, and now his stubborn heart is conquered by a sweet violence.

4. It is a high calling. *I press toward the mark for the prize of the high calling of God in Christ Jesus* (Philippians 3:14). It is a high calling because we are called to high exercises of the Christian religion – to die to sin, to be crucified to the world, to live by faith, and to have fellowship with the Father (1 John 1:3). This is a high calling. This is a work too high for people in a state of nature to perform. It is a high calling because we are called to high privileges – to justification and adoption, to be made co-heirs with Christ. He who is effectually called is higher than the princes of the earth.

5. It is a gracious call. It is the fruit and product of free grace. That God should call some and not others; that some are taken and others are left; that one is called who is of a more rugged, solemn disposition, while another of sharper intellect and sweeter temperament is rejected – here is free grace. That the poor would be *rich in faith, and heirs of the kingdom* (James 2:5), and the nobles and great ones of the world are for the most part rejected – *not many mighty, not many noble, are called* (1 Corinthians 1:26) – this is free and rich grace. *Even so, Father: for so it seemed good in thy sight* (Matthew 11:26). That under the same sermon one person would be powerfully worked upon, while another person would be no more moved than a dead man with the sound of music; that one person would hear the Spirit's voice in the Word, and another not hear it; that one person would be softened and moved with the influence of heaven, while another, like Gideon's dry fleece, has no dew upon him – behold, here is distinguishing grace! The same affliction converts one person and hardens another. Affliction to one person is as the crushing of spices, which casts forth a fragrant smell; to another person it is as the crushing of weeds in a mortar, which are more unsavory. What is the cause of this

except the free grace of God? It is a gracious calling; it is all overlaid and interwoven with free grace.

6. It is a glorious call. *Who hath called us unto his eternal glory by Christ Jesus* (1 Peter 5:10). We are called to the enjoyment of the ever-blessed God, as if a man were called out of a prison to sit upon a throne. Quintus Curtius wrote of someone who, while digging in his garden, was called to be king. Thus God calls us *to glory and virtue* (2 Peter 1:3). First to virtue, then to glory. At Athens there were two temples – the temple of Virtue and the temple of Honor; and no man could go to the temple of Honor except through the temple of Virtue. So God calls us first to virtue, and then to glory. What is the glory among men, which most people so much pursue, but a feather blown in the air? What is it compared to the *weight of glory* (2 Corinthians 4:17)? Is there not much reason for us to follow God's call? He calls us to betterment; can there be any loss or harm in this? God does not want us to part with anything for Him except that which will damn us if we keep it. He has no intention for us except to make us happy. He calls us to salvation. He calls us to a kingdom. Oh, how we should, then, with Bartimaeus, throw off our tattered coat of sin and follow Christ when He calls!

7. It is a rare call. Not many people are savingly called. *Few are chosen* (Matthew 22:14). Few – not collectively, but comparatively. "To call" signifies to choose out some from among others. Many have the light brought to them, but few have their eyes anointed to see that light. *Thou hast a few names even in Sardis which have not defiled their garments* (Revelation 3:4). How many millions sit in the region of darkness! And in those climates where the Sun

of righteousness does shine, there are many who receive the light of the truth without the love of it. There are many religionists, but few believers. There is something that looks like faith that is not true faith. Pliny said that the Cyprian diamond sparkles like a true diamond, but it is not of the right kind; it will break with the hammer. In the same way, the hypocrite's faith will break with the hammer of persecution. Only a few are truly called. The number of precious stones is few compared to the number of pebbles. Most people shape their religion according to the fashion of the times; they are for the music and the idol (Daniel 3:7). The serious thought of this should make us work out our salvation with fear (Philippians 2:12) and strive to be in the number of those few whom God has transformed into a state of grace.

8. It is an unchangeable call. *The gifts and calling of God are without repentance* (Romans 11:29). That is, as a learned writer says, those gifts that flow from election. When God calls someone, He does not repent of it. God does not, as many friends do, love someone one day and hate the person another day; or as princes, who make their subjects favorites and afterward throw them into prison. This is the blessedness of a saint; his condition allows no alteration. God's call is founded upon His decree, and His decree is immutable. Acts of grace cannot be reversed. God blots out His people's sins, but not their names. The world may bring changes every hour, but a believer's condition is fused and unalterable.

6. The purpose of our effectual calling is the honor of God. *That we should be to the praise of his glory* (Ephesians 1:12). He

who is in the state of nature is no more fit to honor God than a beast is to put forth acts of reason. A person before conversion continually reflects dishonor upon God. As dark mists that arise out of swampy, boggy ground cloud and darken the sun, so dark vapors of sin arise out of the natural man's heart and cast a cloud upon God's glory. The sinner is skilled in treason, but understands nothing of loyalty to the King of heaven. But there are some upon whom the lot of free grace falls, and these will be taken as jewels from among the rubbish and will be effectually called so that they may lift up God's name in the world. The Lord will have some people in all ages who will oppose the corruptions of the times, bear witness to His truths, and convert sinners from the error of their ways. He will have His worthy men, as king David had (2 Samuel 23; 1 Chronicles 11). Those who have been monuments of God's mercies will be trumpets of His praise.

These considerations show us the necessity of effectual calling. Without it, there is no going to heaven. We must be made fit for the inheritance (Colossians 1:12). As God makes heaven fit for us, so He makes us fit for heaven; and what makes us fit for this except effectual calling? A man remaining in the filth and rubbish of nature is no more fit for heaven than a dead man is fit to inherit an estate. The high calling is not something arbitrary or indifferent, but is as needful as salvation; yet sadly, how this one thing needful is neglected! Most people, like the people of Israel, wander up and down to gather straw, but do not take heed to the evidences of their effectual calling.

Take notice what a mighty power God puts forth in calling sinners! God so calls as to draw us to Him (John 6:44). Conversion is described as a resurrection. *Blessed and holy is he that hath part in the first resurrection* (Revelation 20:6). That is, it is a rising from sin to grace. A person can no more convert himself than a dead man can raise himself. It is called a creation (Colossians 3:10). To create is above the power of nature.

Objection: Some people say that the will is not dead, but asleep, and that God, by a moral persuasion, only awakens us, and then the will can obey God's call and move of itself to its own conversion.

Answer: To this I answer that every person is bound in chains by sin. *I perceive that thou art in . . . the bond of iniquity* (Acts 8:23). If you present arguments to a person who is in chains, and persuade him to go, is that enough? No. His chains must be broken and he must be set free before he can walk. So it is with every natural man. He is bound with corruption, and the Lord, by converting grace, must file off his chains and give him legs to run, too, or he can never obtain salvation.

Application: An exhortation to make your calling sure.

Give diligence to make your calling and election sure (2 Peter 1:10). It is the great business of our lives to get sound evidences of our effectual calling. Do not settle for outward privileges. Do not cry as the Jews, *The temple of the* LORD (Jeremiah 7:4). Do not rest in baptism. What good does it do to have the water and lack the Spirit? Do not be content that Christ has been preached to you. Do not satisfy yourselves with an empty profession of faith. You may have all this, yet be no better than blazing comets.

Instead, work to confirm to your souls that you are called of God. Do not be like the Athenians to want to hear news (Acts 17:21). What is the state and bias of the times? What changes are likely to happen in such a year? What does all this matter if you are not effectually called? What if the times would have a fairer aspect? What good would it do you if glory dwelled in our land, but grace did not dwell in your heart? Oh my brethren, when things are dark without, let all be clear within. Give diligence to make your calling sure. It is both possible and probable. God is not lacking to those who seek Him. Do not let this important business hang in hand any longer. If there were a controversy about your land, you would use all means to clear your title; and is salvation nothing? Will you not clear your title here? Consider how sad your case is if you are not effectually called.

You are strangers to God. The prodigal went into a far country (Luke 15:13), which implies that every sinner, before conversion, is far from God. *At that time ye were without Christ, . . . strangers from the covenants of promise* (Ephesians 2:12). People dying in their sins have no more right to promises than strangers have to the privilege of free-born citizens. If you are strangers, what language can you expect from God, other than this: *I never knew you* (Matthew 7:23)?

If you are not effectually called, you are enemies: *alienated and enemies* (Colossians 1:21). There is nothing in the Bible you can lay claim to other than the threatenings. You are heirs to all the plagues written in the book of God. Though you may resist the commands of the law, you cannot flee from the curses of the law. Those who are enemies to God, let them read their doom: *But those mine enemies, which would not that I should reign over them, bring hither, and slay them before me* (Luke 19:27). Oh, how it should concern you, therefore, to make your calling sure! How miserable and damnable your condition will be if death calls you before the Spirit calls you!

Question: But is there any hope of my being called? I have been a great sinner.

Answer: Great sinners have been called. Paul was a persecutor, yet he was called. Some of the Jews who had a hand in crucifying Christ were called. God loves to display His free grace to sinners. Therefore, do not be discouraged. You see a golden cord let down from heaven for poor trembling souls to lay hold upon.

Question: But how will I know that I am effectually called?

Answer: He who is savingly called is called out of himself, not only out of sinful self, but out of righteous self. He rejects trust in his duties and moral qualities. *Not having mine own righteousness* (Philippians 3:9). He whose heart God has touched by His Spirit lays down the idol of self-righteousness at Christ's feet for Him to tread upon. He uses morality and duties of piety, but does not trust in them. Noah's dove made use of her wings to fly, but trusted in the ark for safety. It is an excellent thing when a man is called out of himself. As Augustine said, this self-renunciation is the first step to saving faith.

Noah's dove made use of her wings to fly, but trusted in the ark for safety.

He who is effectually called has a visible change worked upon him. It is not a change of the abilities, but of the qualities. He is changed from what he was before. His body is the same, but not his mind; he has another spirit. Paul was so changed after his conversion that people did not know him (Acts 9:21). Oh, what a metamorphosis grace makes! *And such were some of you: but ye are washed, but ye are sanctified, but ye are justified in the name of the Lord Jesus, and by the Spirit of our God* (1 Corinthians 6:11). Grace changes the heart.

In effectual calling, there is a threefold change brought about.

1. There is a change brought about in the understanding. Before, there was ignorance. Darkness was upon the face of the deep, but now there is light. *Now are ye light in the Lord* (Ephesians 5:8). The first work of God in the creation

of the world was light, and so it is in the new creation. He who is savingly called says with that man in the gospel, *Whereas I was blind, now I see* (John 9:25). He sees such evil in sin, and such excellency in the ways of God, that he never saw before. Indeed, this light that the blessed Spirit brings may well be called a marvelous light. *That ye should show forth the praises of Him who hath called you out of darkness into his marvellous light* (1 Peter 2:9).

It is a marvelous light in six respects. (1) Because it is marvelously manifested. It does not come from the celestial orbs where the planets are, but from the Sun of righteousness. (2) It is marvelous in the effect. This light does that which no other light can. It makes a person perceive himself to be blind. (3) It is a marvelous light because it is more penetrating. Other light may shine upon the face, but this light shines into the heart and enlightens the conscience (2 Corinthians 4:6). (4) It is a marvelous light because it causes those who have it to marvel. They marvel at themselves – how could they have been content to be so long without it? They marvel that their eyes would be opened, and not others. They marvel that even though they hated and opposed this light, yet it shined in the firmament of their souls. This is what the saints will stand wondering at to all eternity. (5) It is a marvelous light because it is more vibrant than any other. It not only enlightens, but it makes alive those who *were dead in trespasses and sins* (Ephesians 2:1). Therefore, it is called *the light of life* (John 8:12). (6) It is a marvelous light because it is the beginning of everlasting light. The light of grace is the morning star that ushers in the sunlight of glory.

Now then, reader, can you say that this marvelous light of

the Spirit has dawned upon you? When you were enclosed in ignorance and did not know God or yourself, did a light from heaven suddenly shine all around you? This is one part of that blessed change that is brought about in the effectual calling.

2. There is a change brought about in the will. *To will is present with me* (Romans 7:18). The will, which before opposed Christ, now embraces Him. The will, which was an iron sinew, is now like melting wax. It freely receives the stamp and impression of the Holy Spirit. The will moves heavenward and carries all the spheres of the affections along with it. The regenerate will answers to every call of God, as the echo answers to the voice. *Lord, what wilt thou have me to do?* (Acts 9:6). The will now becomes a volunteer, and it enlists itself under the Captain of salvation (Hebrews 2:10). Oh, what a happy change is brought about here! Before, the will kept Christ out; now it keeps sin out.

   Before, the will kept Christ out; now it keeps sin out.

3. There is a change brought about in the conduct. He who is called of God walks directly contrary to what he did before. Before, he walked in envy and malice, but now he walks in love. Before, he walked in pride, but now he walks in humility. The direction of flow is carried quite another way. As there is a new birth in the hearth, so there is a new version in the life. Thus we see what a mighty change is brought about in those who are called of God.

How far they are from this effectual call who never had any change! They are the same as they were forty or fifty years ago. They are as proud and carnal as ever. They have seen many changes in their times, but they have had no change in their hearts. Do not let people think that they can leap out of the harlot's lap (the world) and into Abraham's bosom; they must have either a gracious change while they live, or a cursed change when they die.

He who is called of God esteems this call as the highest blessing. A king whom God has called by His grace values it more that he is called to be a saint than that he is called to be a king. He values his high calling more than his high birth. Theodosius thought it was a greater honor to be a Christian than to be an emperor. A carnal person can no more value spiritual blessings than a baby can value a diamond necklace. He prefers his worldly splendor – his ease, plenty, and titles of honor – above conversion. He would rather be called a duke than a saint; that is a sign that he is a stranger to effectual calling. He who is enlightened by the Spirit considers holiness his best insignia, and looks upon his effectual calling as his advancement. When he truly begins to think in this way, he is a candidate for heaven.

He who is effectually called is called out of the world. It is a *heavenly calling* (Hebrews 3:1). He who is called of God cares for heavenly things. He is in the world, but not of the world. Naturalists say that although precious stones have their matter from the earth, yet their sparkling luster is from the influence of the heavens. It is the same with a godly man; although his body is from the earth, yet the sparkling of his affections is from heaven. His heart is drawn into the upper region, as high as Christ. He not only casts off every wicked work, but every earthly weight. He is not a worm, but an eagle.

Another sign of our effectual calling is diligence in our normal duties and occupations. Some people boast of their high calling, but they lie idly at anchor. The Christian religion does not approve of idleness. Christians must not be slothful. Idleness is the devil's bath; a slothful person becomes a prey to every temptation. Grace, while it cures the heart, does not make the hand lame. As the person who is called of God works for heaven, so he works in his trade.

Chapter 8

Exhortations to Those
Who Are Called

If, after searching, you find that you are effectually called, I have three exhortations to you.

1. Admire and adore God's free grace in calling you – that God would pass over so many people, that He would pass by the wise and noble, and that the lot of free grace would fall upon you! Be amazed and grateful that He would take you out of a state of bondage, from grinding the devil's mill, and would set you above the princes of the earth and call you to inherit the throne of glory! Fall upon your knees and break forth into a thankful triumph of praise. Let your hearts be ten-stringed instruments to sound forth the memorial of God's mercy (Psalm 33:2; 92:3; 144:9). There is no one as deep in debt to free grace as you, and no one should be so highly mounted upon the pinnacle of thanksgiving. Say as the sweet singer, *I will extol thee, my God, O king; and I will bless thy name for ever and ever. Every day will I bless thee; and I will praise thy name for ever and ever* (Psalm 145:1-2). Those who are patterns

of mercy should be trumpets of praise. Oh, long to be in heaven, where your thanksgivings will be purer and will be raised a note higher.

2. Pity those who are not yet called. Sinners in scarlet are not objects of envy, but pity. They are under *the power of Satan* (Acts 26:18). They tread every day on the brink of the bottomless pit; and what if death would cast them in! Oh, pity unconverted sinners! If you pity an ox or a donkey going astray, will you not pity a soul going astray from God, who has lost his way and his sense, and is upon the precipice of damnation?

   Do not just pity sinners, but pray for them. Though they curse, you must pray. You will pray for senseless and irrational people, and sinners are senseless and irrational. *When he came to himself* (Luke 15:17). It seems that the prodigal before conversion was not himself. Wicked people are going to execution. Sin is the rope that strangles them, death knocks them off the ladder, and hell is their burning place; and will you not pray for them when you see them in such danger?

3. You who are effectually called, honor your high calling. *I, therefore, . . . beseech you that you walk worthy of the vocation wherewith you are called* (Ephesians 4:1). Christians must keep respectability. They must observe what is decent. This is timely advice, when many who profess to be called of God cast a blemish on religion by their loose and inconsistent lives, whereby the ways of God are evil spoken of. Salvian said, "What do pagans say when they see Christians live scandalously? Surely Christ taught them no better." Will you reproach Christ and make Him suffer again by abusing your heavenly calling? It is one of the saddest sights to see someone lift

up his hands in prayer, and with those hands oppress; to hear the same tongue praise God at one time, and lie and slander at another; to hear a person profess God in words, and in works deny Him. Oh, how unworthy this is! Yours is a holy calling, and will you be unholy? Do not think you may take liberty as others do. The Nazarite who had a vow on him separated himself to God and promised to abstain from wine. Although others drank wine, it was not right for the Nazarite to do so. In the same way, although others are loose and vain, it is not right for those who are set apart for God by effectual calling. Are not flowers sweeter than weeds? You must be now *a peculiar people* (1 Peter 2:9) – not only peculiar in regard to dignity, but also in regard to conduct. Abhor all actions and appearances of sin, because it would discredit your high calling.

A true saint is for precise obedience; he follows the canon of Scripture.

Question: What does it mean to walk worthy of our heavenly calling?

Answer: It is to walk consistently, to tread with an even foot, and to walk according to the rules and principles of the Word. A true saint is for precise obedience; he follows the canon of Scripture. *As many as walk according to this rule* (Galatians 6:16). When we leave men's inventions and cling to God's rules; when we walk after the Word, as Israel walked after the pillar of fire – this is walking worthy of our heavenly calling.

To walk worthy of our calling is to walk individually. Noah was upright and righteous in his generation (Genesis 6:9; 7:1). When others walked with the devil, Noah walked with God. We are forbidden to run with the multitude (Exodus 23:2).

Although in civil things individuality is not commendable, yet in the Christian religion it is good to be different from others. Melanchthon was the glory of the age he lived in. Athanasius was individually holy. He appeared for God when the stream of the times ran another way. It is better to be a pattern of holiness than a partner in wickedness. It is better to go to heaven with a few than to go to hell in the crowd. We must walk in an opposite way to the people of the world.

To walk worthy of our calling is to walk cheerfully. *Rejoice in the Lord always* (Philippians 4:4). Too much sadness of spirit discredits our high calling and makes others suspect a godly life to be gloomy. Christ loves to see us rejoicing in Him. Causinus, in his hieroglyphics, speaks of a dove, whose wings being perfumed with sweet ointments, drew the other doves after her. Cheerfulness is a perfume to draw others to godliness. True religion does not banish all joy. As there is a seriousness without irritability, so there is a cheerful liveliness without frivolity. When the prodigal was converted, *they began to be merry* (Luke 15:24). Who should be cheerful if not the people of God? They are no sooner born of the Spirit but they are heirs to a crown. God is their portion and heaven is their mansion, and should they not rejoice?

To walk worthy of our calling is to walk wisely. Walking wisely implies three things:

1. To walk cautiously. *The wise man's eyes are in his head* (Ecclesiastes 2:14). Others watch for our faltering; therefore, we had better look to our situation. We must beware not only of scandals, but of all that is improper, lest thereby we open the mouths of others with a fresh cry against Christianity. If our piety will not convert people, our prudence may silence them.

2. To walk courteously. The spirit of the gospel is full of

meekness and honor. *Be courteous* (1 Peter 3:8). Take heed of a sour, superior behavior. True religion does not take away civility, but refines it. *Abraham stood up, and bowed himself to the people of the land* (Genesis 23:7). Though they were of a heathen race, yet Abraham gave them a civil respect. Paul was of a gracious temperament. *I am made all things to all men, that I might by all means save some* (1 Corinthians 9:22). In lesser matters, the apostle yielded to others so that by his gracious manner, he might win them over.

3. To walk honorably. Though we must be humble, we do not need to be subservient. It is unworthy to sacrifice ourselves to the lusts of men. What is sinfully imposed ought to be zealously opposed. Conscience is God's jurisdiction, where no one has the right to visit except He who is the Bishop of our souls (1 Peter 2:25). We must not be like hot iron, which may be beaten into any form. A brave-spirited Christian will rather suffer than let his conscience be violated. Here is the serpent and the dove united – wisdom and innocence (Matthew 10:16). This wise walking agrees with our high calling, and does not a little adorn the gospel of Christ.

To walk worthy of our calling is to walk influentially – to do good to others and to be rich in acts of mercy (Hebrews 13:16). Good works honor true religion. As Mary poured the ointment on Christ, so by good works we pour ointments on the head of the gospel and make it give forth a fragrant smell. Good works, although they are not causes of salvation, yet they are evidences of it. When with our Saviour we go about doing good, and send abroad the refreshing influence of our kindness, we walk worthy of our high calling.

This is a matter of consolation to you who are effectually

called. God has magnified rich grace toward you. You are called to great honor to be co-partners with the angels, and co-heirs with Christ (Romans 8:17). This should revive you in the worst of times. So what if people reproach and insult you? Set God's calling of you against their miscalling. So what if people persecute you to death? They only give you a pass and send you to heaven sooner. How this may cure the trembling of the heart! So what if the sea roars, the earth trembles, and the stars are shaken out of their places? You do not need to fear (Psalm 46:1-3). You are called, and therefore you are sure to be crowned.

Chapter 9

Concerning God's Purpose

1. God's purpose is the cause of salvation.

The third and last thing in the text, which I will only briefly discuss, is the ground and origin of our effectual calling, in these words: *according to [His] purpose* (Ephesians 1:11). Anselm rendered it, "According to His good will." Peter Martyr showed it as "According to His decree." This purpose, or decree, of God is the fountainhead of our spiritual blessings. It is the impulsive cause of our vocation, justification, and glorification. It is the highest link in the golden chain of salvation. What is the reason that one person is called, and not another? It is from the eternal purpose of God. God's decree gives the casting voice in man's salvation.

Let us then ascribe the whole work of grace to the desire of God's will. God did not choose us because we were worthy, but by choosing us He makes us worthy. Proud people are inclined to assume and claim too much to themselves in being sharers with God. While many people cry out against church sacrilege, they are in the meantime guilty of a far greater sacrilege – that of robbing God of His glory while they go to set the crown of salvation upon their own head. But we must resolve all into

God's purpose. The signs of salvation are in the saints, but the cause of salvation is in God.

If it is God's purpose that saves, then it is not free will. Pelagians strongly proclaim and assert free will. They tell us that a person has an innate power to bring about his own conversion; but this text disproves it. Our calling is "according to God's purpose." The Scripture pulls up the root of free will. *It is not of him that willeth* (Romans 9:16). Everything depends upon the purpose of God. When the prisoner is sentenced by the judge, there is no saving him unless the king has a purpose to save him. God's purpose is His royal prerogative.

If it is God's purpose that saves, then it is not merit. Bellarmine held that good works make amends for sin and merit glory, but *If it is God's purpose that saves, then it is not merit.* the text says that we are called according to God's purpose. There is also a parallel verse: *Who hath saved us, and called us with an holy calling, not according to our works, but according to his own purpose and grace* (2 Timothy 1:9). There is no such thing as merit. Our best works have in them both defection and infection, and so are only glittering sins; therefore, if we are called and justified, it is God's purpose that brings it to pass.

Objection: But the Roman Catholics allege the following verse for support: *Henceforth there is laid up for me a crown of righteousness, which the Lord, the righteous judge, shall give me at that day* (2 Timothy 4:8). This is the force of their argument. If God in justice rewards our works, then they merit salvation.

Reply: To this I answer that God gives a reward as a just Judge not to the worthiness of our works, but to the worthiness of Christ. God as a just Judge rewards us not because we have deserved it, but because He has promised it. God has two courts:

a court of mercy and a court of justice. The Lord condemns those works in the court of justice that He crowns in the court of mercy. Therefore, that which carries the main pulse in our salvation is the purpose of God.

Again, if the purpose of God is the springhead of happiness, then we are not saved for faith foreseen. It is absurd to think that anything in us could have the least influence upon our election. Some people say that God did foresee that certain people would believe, and therefore did choose them. Therefore, they make the business of salvation to depend upon something in us. Whereas God does not choose us *for* faith, but *to* faith. *He hath chosen us . . . that we should be holy* (Ephesians 1:4). He did not choose us because we wanted to be holy, but that we might be holy. We are elected *to* holiness, not because of it. What could God foresee in us except pollution and rebellion? If anyone is saved, it is according to God's purpose.

Question: How will we know that God has a purpose to save us?

Answer: By being effectually called. *Give diligence to make your calling and election sure* (2 Peter 1:10). We make our election sure by making our calling sure. *God hath from the beginning chosen you to salvation through sanctification of the Spirit and belief of the truth* (2 Thessalonians 2:13). By the stream, we come at last to the fountain. If we find the stream of sanctification running in our souls, we may by this come to the springhead of election. When a person cannot look up to the ornament, yet he may know that the moon is there by seeing it shine upon the water. In the same way, although I cannot look up into the secret of God's purpose, yet I may know that I am elected by the shining of sanctifying grace in my soul. Whosoever finds the Word of God transcribed and copied out into his heart may undeniably conclude his election.

2. God's purpose is the ground of assurance.

This is a sovereign tonic of unspeakable comfort to those who are the called of God. Their salvation rests upon God's purpose. *The foundation of God standeth sure, having this seal, The Lord knoweth them that are his. And, Let everyone that nameth the name of Christ depart from iniquity* (2 Timothy 2:19). Our graces are imperfect, and our comforts ebb and flow, but God's foundation stands sure. Those who are built upon this rock of God's eternal purpose do not need to fear falling away; neither the power of man nor the force of temptation will ever be able to overturn them.

Thomas Watson
– A Brief Biography

Thomas Watson (c. 1620-1686) was an English Nonconformist Puritan pastor and author. He earned his Bachelor of Arts and Master of Arts degrees from Emmanuel College, Cambridge. In 1646 Watson was employed at St. Stephen Walbrook Church in London, where he remained for the next sixteen years.

Thomas married Abigail Beadle in about 1647, and they had at least seven children, although four of the children died when young. During the English Civil War (1642-1649), Watson leaned toward Presbyterian views, and he sided with the Presbyterians in opposition to the death of King Charles I.

Watson was imprisoned in 1651 for his part in a plot to bring back Charles II.

In 1652 Watson was released from prison and returned to his duties at St. Stephen Walbrook Church. After the Act of Uniformity was passed in 1662, Watson, a Nonconformist, could no longer preach there, although he continued preaching in private when he was able. After the Declaration of Indulgence was passed in 1672, Thomas Watson was able to obtain a license to preach at Crosby Hall in London. He continued preaching there until his health began to decline. He then retired to Barnston in Essex, where he died in 1686 while praying.

Thomas Watson's notable writings include *The Godly Man's Picture*, *The Ten Commandments*, *Heaven Taken by Storm*, *The Doctrine of Repentance*, *The Beatitudes*, *The Lord's Prayer*, and *The Body of Divinity*.

Thomas Watson lived his life for God, and he fit his own definition of a true Christian. Watson wrote that "A true Christian carries Christ in his heart and the cross on his shoulders." Watson had his share of difficulty and sorrow, yet he remained a good soldier of Jesus Christ. He believed what he preached and wrote, and he lived what he believed.

> *"Soon the battle will be over. It will not be long before the day will come when Satan will no longer trouble us. There will be no more deception, temptation, accusation, or confrontation. Our warfare will be over and our commander, Jesus Christ, will call us away from the battlefield to receive the victor's crown." – Thomas Watson*

Other Similar Titles

The Beatitudes,
by Thomas Watson

The sermon on the mount is full of sweet variety. It is a piece of spiritual needlework that is worked throughout with various colors. This is both useful and pleasant. In this portion of Holy Scripture, you have a synopsis of the Christian religion. You have the Bible summarized. There is a garden of delight in this sermon. It is set with special growths where you may pick those flowers that will enrich the hidden man of your heart. In this sermon, you find the golden key that will open the gate of Paradise. It contains the channel of the gospel through which runs wine to sustain those who are poor in spirit and pure in heart. It is the rich cabinet in which the Pearl of Blessedness is locked up. It is the golden pot that contains the manna that will feed and refresh the soul unto everlasting life. It is a pathway that leads to the Holy of Holies.

Available where books are sold.

The Art of Divine Contentment,
by Thomas Watson

The contented heart is never out of heart. Contentment is a golden shield that beats back discouragement. True contentment will trust God even when it cannot see Him. Why are you discontented? Is it because you are temporarily dispossessed of comforts? You who are discontented because you do not have all you would like to have, let me tell you, either your faith is a nonentity, or, at best, it is just an embryo. It is a weak faith that must have stilts and crutches to support it.

Discontent is not only below faith, but it is also below reason. Discontent is unworthy of the relationship we have with God. Christians are invested with the title and privilege of sonship; we are heirs of the promise. God will be sure to reward the contented Christian.

Available where books are sold.

The Doctrine of Repentance,
by Thomas Watson

Repentance is not optional. It is not left to our choice whether or not we will repent, but it is an indispensable command. God has enacted a law in the High Court of heaven that no sinner will be saved except the repenting sinner, and he will not break his own law. No one can willfully continue in sin and expect to be covered by the blood of Christ. Even if all the angels stood before God and begged for the life of an unrepenting person, God would not grant it. *The Lord God, compassionate and merciful, . . . who keeps faithfulness for thousands, . . . will by no means leave the guilty unpunished* (Exodus 34:6-7). Though God is more full of mercy than the sun is of light, still He will not forgive a sinner who willfully continues to sin.

Therefore let us, while we are on this side of the grave, make our peace with God!

Available where books are sold.

The Godly Man's Picture,
by Thomas Watson

Here in this book, you have a godly person's portrait, and you see him portrayed in his full qualities and features. What a rare thing godliness is! Godliness is a ray and beam that shines from God. If God is true, then godliness is true. Genuine godliness is not light and fluffy, but it is solid and will engage the heart and spirit.

Christian, aspire after piety; it is a lawful ambition. Look at the saints' characteristics here, and never stop until you have got those same characteristics stamped upon your own soul.

Available where books are sold.

The Godly Man's Picture,
by Thomas Watson

Here in this book, you have a godly person's portrait, and you see him portrayed in his full qualities and features. What a rare thing godliness is! Godliness is a ray and beam that shines from God. If God is true, then godliness is true. Genuine godliness is not light and fluffy, but it is solid and will engage the heart and spirit.

Christian, aspire after piety; it is a lawful ambition. Look at the saints' characteristics here, and never stop until you have got those same characteristics stamped upon your own soul.

Available where books are sold.